The General from America

Richard Nelson's plays include *New England* (RSC, Manhattan Theatre Club), *Misha's Party* (co-written with Alexander Gelman for the Royal Shakespeare Company and the Moscow Art Theatre), *Columbus and the Discovery of Japan* (RSC), *Two Shakespearean Actors* (RSC, Lincoln Center Theatre), *Some Americans Abroad* (RSC, Lincoln Center Theatre), *Sensibility and Sense* (American Playhouse Television), *Principia Scriptoriae* (RSC, Manhattan Theatre Club), *Between East and West, Life Sentences, The Return of Pinocchio, Rip Van Winkle or The Works, The Vienna Notes* and *An American Comedy*. Radio plays include *Languages Spoken Here* (BBC Radio 3), *Eating Words* (Radio 4 and the World Service), *Roots in Water* (Radio 3), *Advice to Eastern Europe* (Radio 4) and *The American Wife* (Radio 3). He has written a television play, *End of a Sentence* (American Playhouse), and a film, *Ethan Frome*. Among his awards are the prestigious Lila Wallace Readers' Digest Award in 1991, a London *Time Out* award, two Obies, two Giles Cooper Awards, a Guggenheim Fellowship, two Rockefeller playwriting grants and two National Endowment for the Arts playwriting fellowships. He is an Honorary Asssociate Artist of the RSC.

Making Plays – The Writer–Director Relationship in the Theatre Today, co-written by David Jones and edited by Colin Chambers, was published in 1995 by Faber and Faber.

RICHARD NELSON

The General
from America

faber and faber
LONDON · BOSTON

First published in 1996
by Faber and Faber Limited
3 Queen Square London WC1N 3AU

Photoset by Parker Typesetting Service, Leicester
Printed in England by Clays Ltd, St Ives plc

A CIP record for this book
is available from the British Library
ISBN 0-571-19018-9

2 4 6 8 10 9 7 5 3 1

For Robert Marx

Characters

Benedict Arnold
Peggy Arnold, his wife
Hannah Arnold, his sister
Major John Andre
Sir Henry Clinton
Alexander Hamilton
General George Washington
Major Stephen Kemble

Joseph Reed
Timothy Matlack
Colonel Simcoe
Young Woman behind the Curtain
Mrs Henry Clinton
Van Wart, a skinner
Pauling, a skinner
Minister
Woman from the Choir
Officers, orderlies, pallbearers, etc.
The smaller roles are written to be doubled.

The following is based on true events.

The General from America was first performed by the Royal Shakespeare Company on 17 July 1996 at the Swan Theatre, Stratford-on-Avon. The cast was as follows:

Benedict Arnold James Laurenson
Peggy Arnold Jay McInnes
Hannah Arnold Rachel Joyce
John Andre Adam Godley
Sir Henry Clinton John Woodvine
Alexander Hamilton David Tennant
George Washington Corin Redgrave
Major Kemble Stephen Boxer
Joseph Reed Benny Young
Colonel Simcoe Nathaniel Duncan
Young Woman Jacquelyn Yorke
Mrs Clinton Jan Chappell
Van Wart Simeon Defoe
Pauling Andrew Hesker
Matlack Jon Rake
Robinson Owen Oakeshott
Maid Emma Poole
Other parts played by members of the company.

Directed by Howard Davies
Designed by William Dudley
Lighting designed by Mark Henderson
Music by Ilona Sekacz
Fights by Terry King
Sound by Martin Slavin
Music Director Michael Tubbs

Assistant Director Simon Nicholson
Dialect work by Joan Washington
Company voice work by Andrew Wade and
  Barbara Houseman

Stage Manager Maggie Mackay
Deputy Stage Manager Rosalind Morgan-Jones
Assistant Stage Manager Joyce Green

SCENE ONE

Philadelphia. 1779. A public square. Night.

A drum roll, and a few men carrying lanterns enter, followed by the drummer. Upstage, in the shadows, a man has been hanged from a tree or scaffold.

Two of the men are Joseph Reed, forties, President of Pennsylvania, and Timothy Matlack, Secretary of the Committee of Pennsylvania. They face an (unseen) crowd.

Reed (*to the crowd*) Quiet! Quiet!

The crowd does not quieten down. Reed turns to the drummer, who then plays a drum roll which quiets the crowd.

(*addressing the crowd*) This man . . .

Gestures behind him, then looks to Matlack who quickly whispers the man's name.

John Roberts, having been tried and convicted of loyalist sympathies, of corresponding with the enemy, of corruption and other crimes against the Commonwealth, has been duly hanged as a spy.

A few cheers from the crowd.

The Committee of Pennsylvania, as the legitimate representative of the people, lays legal claim to all Roberts's properties, and monies and accepts Roberts's widow and –

He turns back to Matlack, who whispers, then:

– ten children into its bosom, wards of the state. May God

have mercy upon them. And may the Lord find the food to feed them.

Reed steps back. Another drum roll. Matlack steps forward, a list in hand.

Matlack (*reading from the list*) By the action of the Committee, three more dwellings have been cleared. Space in these comfortable houses will be assigned to homeless families by lottery. (*then next on the list*) Sick women and children are now to be taken only to 27 Market Street. All medicine is now stored there. This to combat the hoarding of medical supplies by some doctors. (*He looks up from his list.*) Hoarding of medicine is a crime punishable by death. (*then next on the list*) The Committee announces the arrival of twelve wagons of grain from the west. Bread rations shall be increased. The amount of increase shall be posted.

He finishes the list, puts it away, looks at Reed, then continues.

The author of the unsigned attack upon the Committee, its President (*nods towards Reed*), and this Commonwealth, which recently appeared in the *Evening Post*, has been revealed. (*Beat.*) His name is Humphreys. Mr Whitehead Humphreys. He resides, I believe, on Front Street. Number 12.

Matlack is now finished, he turns to the drummer, who gives another roll.

Reed (*over the roll, to the crowd*) Cut him down! (*He points to the hanged man.*) Drag him through our streets! Let him be stoned and spat upon! By those he has betrayed!

Matlack (*turns back and cries*) Cut him down!

Drum roll continues as Reed and Matlack hurry off.

British-occupied New York City.

Small room in a British Officers' Club. A small curtained area, to be used as a makeshift stage. A chair. The room is fairly dark.

Sir Henry Clinton, 50, Commander-in-Chief of the British Army in North America, sits in the chair facing the 'stage'. Around him are three officers. They watch a recitation of a poem written and performed by Major John Andre, 29, a deputy adjutant general. All drink and smoke.

Andre stands before the curtain, reading the poem, which is called 'The Frantic Lover'.

Andre
And shall then another embrace thee my Fair!
Must envy still add to the pangs of Despair!
Shall I live to behold the reciprocal bliss!
Death, death is a refuge, Elysium to this!

Officer He must be talking about New York.

Laughter.
Andre nods to an Orderly by the stage, who now pulls open the curtain. One Officer sh-shs the others.
A Young Woman is revealed. She stands in a tableau vivant which has some relation to the poem being read. After a moment, the curtain closes and Andre continues.

Andre
The star of the evening now bids thee retire
Accurs'd be its Orb and extinguished its fire!
For it shows me my rival prepared to invade
Those charms which at once I admired and obey'd.
Far off each forbidding Incumbrance is thrown
And Sally thy beauties no more are thy own.

Another nod to the Orderly, the curtain is opened, and the Young Woman is in another tableau vivant – though she has now taken off some of her clothes.

Pause. No one says anything. Only Sir Henry turns away and watches Andre instead of the stage. The curtain closes and Andre continues.

Thy coyness too flies as love brings to thy View
A frame more ecstatic than Saint ever knew!
And yet I behold thee tho' longing to die
Approach the new Heaven with a tear and a sigh!
For oh! the fond sigh midst Enjoyment will stray,
And a Tear is the Tribute which Rapture must pay.
Still, still dost thou tremble that pleasure to seek,
Which pants in thy Bosom and glows in they cheek.

Curtain opens. The Young Woman is now naked above the waist, and again in a pose.

No one says anything, they watch, except for Sir Henry, who again turns back to Andre, smiling. Curtain closes.

Here Conquest must pause tho' it ne'er can be cloy'd
To view the rich plunder of beauty enjoy'd,
The tresses dishevelled, the Bosom display'd,
And the Wishes of Years in a moment repaid.
A Thousand soft thoughts in thy fancy combine
A Thousand wild horrors assemble in Mine;
Relieve me kind death, shut the Scene from my View,
And Save me, oh save me, ere madness ensue!

The curtain opens one last time, and the Young Woman is now completely naked. In a melodramatic pose, she now holds a sword, a British flag, and she wears on her head a British officer's hat.

Pause.

Again silence for a while. Andre and Clinton share a smile as the other Officers watch the stage. Finally the

*curtain closes, Andre folds the paper he has been
reading from – the show is over; everyone suddenly
relaxes, though no one knows what to say. An awkward
pause.*

Sir Henry (*finally*) Splendid poem.

*The Officers burst out talking at once and at the same
time, congratulating John, praising him, etc. 'Very nice!'
'I've heard much worse in London.' 'And well
performed!' 'He's quite the actor.' 'I saw him on
Monday in* She Stoops to Conquer.*' 'I want to see that.'
'I saw him last night.'
   The Young Woman comes out from behind the
curtain, a blanket around her shoulders. She hurries out
– this has stopped all conversation as they watch.
   She passes Major Stephen Kemble, who is entering.*

Kemble Sir Henry. If I may have a word.

*An Officer holds up an empty glass: 'Perhaps we should
–' Before he even gets a word out, they are heading off,
to find more to drink, 'We'll be in the next room sir!'
One, nodding in the direction of the Young Woman:
'She's a good actress, don't you think?' 'She'd do well in
London.'
   Kemble stops Andre who is heading out with the
others.*

Major Andre. If you wouldn't mind. This may interest
you.

Andre (*to the Officers*) Get me whatever. I'll catch up.

*The Officers leave, talking. Sir Henry has reached out
and taken Andre's hand.*

Sir Henry What is it, Kemble? (*to Andre*) The men
enjoyed that I think.

5

Andre We need to keep up – their spirits.

Andre and Sir Henry laugh at the joke.

Kemble (*over the laughter*) Sir Henry, we believe we've learned the source of the letter Major Andre received.

Beat.

Andre The man who signs himself 'Monk'?

Kemble (*ignoring Andre*) And we believe – no, we're certain that the writer of the letter, our possible defector, is – General Benedict Arnold –

Andre Jesus Christ.

Kemble (*over this*) – of the Rebel Army. Presently Military Governor of the City of Philadelphia. (*He continues his list.*) Hero of Saratoga. The most decorated and successful officer in the Continental Army.

Sir Henry (*over the end of this*) I know who he is.

Pause. Sir Henry has let go of Andre's hand.

Andre Why would –?

Kemble (*turns to Andre*) Arnold's duty in Philadelphia has been, shall we say, less than rewarding. It's become a mess down there, or so one hears. (*Beat. To Sir Henry*) The man's a bloody good soldier, and it seems a terrible politician. He's being eaten alive. So I suppose it makes some sense for him to test the waters. Which is all I believe the letter attempts to do.

Short pause.

Sir Henry You are sure –?

Kemble nods.

This is extraordinary.

He reaches for and takes Andre's hand again, and holds it now between his two hands.

Kemble Yes, sir. I agree.

Sir Henry (*looking up at Andre*) John . . .

Andre Perhaps their so-called revolution has begun to devour itself. Like you said it would, sir. Congratulations.

Sir Henry It's one man.

Andre The first, sir.

Sir Henry We'll see. Still it's good news.

Kemble I believe we must write back at once, sir, and give him every encouragement.

Sir Henry Yes.

Kemble And promise him? Whatever? (*to Andre*) Sorry, Major, to have interrupted. I understand you're performing now. *She Stoops to Conquer*?

Andre nods.

Good play. (*He turns to Sir Henry.*) By the way, the 'Monk' he signs with we believe refers to a George Monk, General under Cromwell, who changed sides. And for this action received from a grateful sovereign at least a Dukedom. So – I don't suppose he's thinking cheap.

Sir Henry No.

Kemble turns to leave.

Andre (*pulling his hand away from Sir Henry*) One second, Stephen. (*to Sir Henry*) Sir, shouldn't I be the one responding?

Kemble I don't think that's wise –

Sir Henry holds up his hand and cuts Kemble off. He

wants to hear what Andre has to say.

Andre He wrote to me. The letter's to me. It could spook the man if someone else –

Kemble (*interrupting*) He was obviously writing to the Commander-in-Chief. Somehow, maybe through mutual acquaintances in Philadelphia, he'd learned Andre's name. I doubt if –

Andre We don't know that!

Kemble is taken aback by Andre's vehemence.

Kemble You are just a name to get to Sir Henry!

Andre (*over this, to Sir Henry*) Sir, I ask permission to respond to the letter *I* received.

Kemble Sir, Major Andre is not qualified to –

Andre It's my letter!

Kemble I run the service!

Andre Sir Henry?

Kemble General, please!

They both look to Sir Henry.

Sir Henry We must do the cautious thing. Keep it simple. Not get ahead of ourselves. (*Beat.*) A man contemplating this – a general, he must be . . .

Beat. Andre stares at Sir Henry.

John has a point, General Arnold wrote to him.

Kemble Sir, it requires a professional response –

Sir Henry (*over this*) For whatever reason, he did this. We don't know why. And I'm not about to guess. (*He looks at both men.*) It's not a question of rank. You're both . . .

majors. John's now a major. And we know he's a very fine writer.

Kemble I don't see what that has to –

Sir Henry Please, don't interrupt me. (*Beat.*) Arnold must not be scared off. Too many cooks – as they say. Thank you, Major Kemble, I appreciate your hard work. You've done well.

Kemble doesn't move.

I said – thank you.

Andre I'll take the letter, please Stephen.

Kemble hands Andre the letter.

I'll copy you what I write, if you'd like. We're having drinks, if you . . .

Kemble No.

Kemble turns and leaves.
    Andre fiddles with the letter, then holds it up, amazed.

Andre Monk is Benedict Arnold. (*He shakes his head in disbelief.*)

Sir Henry Kemble's probably right – he's just testing the waters. So let's not push him in, John. Wait until he jumps.

Andre I'll do my best.

Sir Henry stands for the first time in the scene, and begins to head off towards the bar.

Sir? Thank you.

Sir Henry stops, looks at Andre.

For once again showing such confidence in me. I owe you so much.

Sir Henry takes a good long look at Andre then smiles, goes to him and puts his arm around him, and gives him a big 'fatherly' hug that is a little too big and lasts a little too long.

He lets him go, looks into Andre's eyes, then with his hand makes a stroke across Andre's cheek.

Sir Henry Just don't disappoint me.

Sir Henry turns and goes out. Andre follows.

SCENE THREE

Garden of the Penn Mansion (Benedict Arnold's residence), Philadelphia. Three chairs. A sunny afternoon.

Arnold, 38, though looking older, enters with Hannah, his sister, 35. Arnold limps on his wounded leg; Hannah helps him to a chair and he sits. Off – sounds of people arriving.

Alexander Hamilton, 23, secretary to George Washington, Joseph Reed, and Peggy Arnold, Benedict's young wife, enter. Peggy is 19, though looks considerably younger, more like 16.

Arnold (*trying to stand*) Colonel Hamilton.

Hamilton (*over this*) Don't get up, please, General.

Arnold (*over this*) How is our Commander-in-Chief?

Hamilton As well as can be expected.

Arnold (*not listening, continues to introduce*) My sister. Colonel Alexander Hamilton. You've met my wife?

Hamilton Yes, just inside –

Arnold (*to Peggy, who is helping Arnold sit back down in the chair*) Colonel Hamilton recently married as well.

Peggy General Schyler's daughter. I know.

Hamilton Who sends regards.

Arnold The daughter does? (*He laughs at his joke, then winks at Peggy.*)

Hamilton (*taken aback*) No, the General does, sir.

Arnold Ahhh! Now that's explained! (*He smiles.*)

Hamilton (*over this*) He is a great admirer. (*He nods towards Arnold.*) You must know that, he tells everyone – you are our greatest field general.

Arnold Look at the competition. That's hardly a compliment.

Hannah We expected you earlier. May I take your hat.

Arnold (*over this, to Peggy*) I've told you about Schyler –

Peggy Like a father to you.

Arnold (*over this, to Hamilton*) What can I get you? Take Mr Hamilton's hat, Hannah.

Peggy Sit down, please.

> *Peggy sits next to Arnold. There is only one remaining chair.*
> *Reed has been completely ignored and stands awkwardly to one side.*

Hamilton (*hesitating to sit*) And Mr Reed?

Arnold (*ignoring him*) You don't mind sitting outside –?

Peggy It's terribly hot in the house.

Hamilton I don't mind. It's lovely. There's a nice breeze.

> *Hamilton, feeling awkward because Reed is left standing, turns to Reed.*

Mr Reed was kind enough to escort me –

Arnold (*turns to Reed*) Mr Reed, are you joining us?

Beat.

Hamilton Is there another chair?

Arnold Peggy, do we have another chair for Mr Reed?

Peggy I don't think so.

Arnold Pity.

Awkward pause.

(*taking Peggy's hand*) Is she as lovely as you've heard, Mr Hamilton?

Hamilton It is our good fortune that I'm now married, sir. (*He laughs.*)

Arnold You're not that handsome. (*He smiles. To Peggy*) Is he?

Peggy I'm sure his new rich wife thinks so.

Hannah Is Mr Reed staying? I'll bring tea. How many cups –?

Reed I came only to deliver Colonel Hamilton. That is now achieved. (*Beat.*) My regards, Colonel, to General Washington –

Arnold (*over the end of this, to Reed*) What crimes do the Committee of Pennsylvania accuse me of today? (*He laughs at his joke, and turns back to the others.*)

Reed That depends – upon what crimes you have committed today, General.

Beat.

Arnold (*to Hamilton*) For him, we sacrifice. We die. It makes no sense. Each morning I wake up and think: am I mad?

Reed You haven't died yet. I keep waiting.

Arnold (*over the end of this*) You arrogant bastard, I gave a leg for you people!

Reed And *that* leg I honour. It's the hand you've got in our pocket that I abhor!

Arnold I am an honest man!

Reed (*to Hamilton*) Read him the charges.

Hamilton Please, I've listened to you! You've had your say!

Reed (*over this*) Tell him what he's done!

Arnold (*nearly bolting to his feet*) What I've done! Where to even begin with what you've done! (*to Hamilton*) Just last night – have you heard what took place last night?

Reed (*over this*) You can't defend the writer!

Hamilton (*to Reed*) What took place last –?

Arnold First the offices of the *Evening Post* were attacked by his thugs.

Reed They are not thugs! They are good citizens of Philadelphia!

Arnold (*over this, continuing*) For publishing an editorial critical of Mr Reed's Committee's effort to seize all women and children of Loyalists who have departed the city.

Peggy (*over this*) I thought he was leaving, we have no more chairs!

Reed (*to Arnold*) We are afraid for their safety.

Arnold Untrue. You want their homes.

Reed We are short of food.

Arnold This is true.

Reed And they are women and children of traitors!

Arnold They are women and children!

Reed (*over this*) People are hungry, look in the streets. If you can get your face out of your own full table!

Arnold (*over the end of this*) My soul is with the people in the streets!

Reed (*to Hamilton*) Control your greed, General! That's all we ask!

Arnold As you attack our newspapers!

Reed An overflow of liberty. Too much vigilance is better than too little. I am a radical, General Arnold. I will not shrink from that.

   Beat.

Arnold And I am not? (*He looks around incredulously.*) Is this not my war too?

Reed You do not wish me to answer that, sir. Mr Hamilton, I've done my duty. I've spoken the truth. I've catalogued the crimes. And I've brought you to the criminal. What more can I do? Good day. Give my regards to our Commander-in-Chief and tell him, I pray for him. Daily. (*He turns and leaves.*)

   Hannah has just entered with the tea.

Hannah Should I show him out?

   Arnold has turned away. Short pause.

Hamilton I'm sorry, but what occurred last night? What – do you think occurred?

Arnold hesitates, hearing the correction, then:

Arnold Thugs – Mr Reed's patriots – broke into the newspaper office I mentioned, which had had the audacity to criticize Mr Reed's Committee – in an unsigned article of course. How brave we've all become.

Hannah has begun to set out the tea. Peggy helps.

They beat the name of the author out of whomever happened to be there. A merchant, a Mr Humphreys, I believe, is the writer. And then an even bigger mob was raised, went to Humphreys' house. He wasn't home, so they beat up his sister instead.

Peggy I know the woman.

Arnold And a boarder, who happened to be a new member of Congress from Georgia. Thus is Mr Reed's – liberty.

Peggy (*to Hamilton*) The woman's a friend of my sister's. Small, frail woman.

Arnold (*sitting back, closing his eyes*) They do not wish a revolution, Mr Hamilton. They wish a civil war. But I am only a soldier. I do only what I'm told. My job now is to shoot Americans as they fight for food in the street.

Short pause. Tea is poured.

Hamilton It will get better.

No response. Then Arnold opens his eyes, leans forward to take his tea.

Arnold (*under his breath*) Will it?

Peggy takes his hand in hers. Silence. No one knows what to say.
Above a flock of geese are heard passing by.
Arnold shifts his weight, he is in some discomfort and

pain. Peggy leans over and slowly lifts his bad leg up with effort. Arnold dramatically waves her off, and then with great effort and pain, and without help, he lifts his wounded leg onto the edge of Peggy's chair.

Hamilton Allow me, sir, to help . . .

Arnold No. I bear my burden alone. I need no help. I have the sin of pride, sir. (*He stifles a groan, then adjusts his position. In pain*) So Reed has accused me of –? I'm sure you'll tell me all.

Hamilton I've spent the morning taking his deposition, yes.

Arnold And what do you think?

Hamilton I'm not here to think, sir. General Washington will review my reports, and he shall decide on the merits of this case. (*Beat.*) I'm here now to learn what you'd like to say. To have in the record. (*Beat.*) We can begin whenever you . . .

Arnold watches the birds, seemingly distracted and uninterested.

Perhaps Mrs Arnold . . .

Arnold (*watching the birds*) My wife will stay. She is my comfort.

Hannah turns to leave.

And my sister. Who has always stood at my side.

Hannah turns back.

Hamilton I understand. (*He begins to set up a lap desk, in preparation for taking notes.*)

Peggy Would you like anything, Colonel?

Hamilton I'm –

16

Arnold (*before he can answer*) I don't know what you want from me. Or what you expect. I am a proud man, forgive me for that. And that is all I shall ask you to forgive me for.

Hamilton (*being handed a cake*) Perhaps if you address –

Arnold (*interrupting*) I cannot plead for my honesty!

Hamilton (*continuing*) If you address the charges. Give us your own explanations. That will be enough.

   Beat. Arnold looks at Peggy, then Hannah, then:

Arnold Go ahead. What is the first charge?

Hamilton (*balancing the cake, and papers, and lap desk*) Mr Reed and the Committee of Pennsylvania claim –

Arnold (*interrupting*) I have killed, I don't know, maybe forty men with these hands, Colonel – in this war. Our war. I have not been a general who stays on the high ground.

Hamilton That is well known. And much admired.

Arnold Six, no seven – with a sword. I know what the English claim, we cannot stand and take a bayonet run. That hasn't been the case with me, has it?

Hamilton No, sir.

Arnold (*turning to the women, who react to the gruesomeness of his story*) The sound, the feel of the blade hitting bone. That's something you don't forget. It's like a – (*He makes the sound.*) And if you hit the bone head on, it pushes you back a bit. Can knock you down. (*He demonstrates – the jerk reaction. To Hamilton*) That's if you plunge. (*He turns to Peggy, who is making faces, reacting to the gore.*) She's a woman. (*to Hamilton*) If you swipe, you want to keep your wrist loose, forget the bone, and slice the muscle. Take the bugger down. Kill him when he's down. They beg with their eyes then. What's the first charge? (*then without letting Hamilton answer*) It was seven. Not six. With the sword. I remember now. He was a boy. The seventh. Plunged it into his Godforsaken face. Ridgefield. The seventh. (*Short pause.*) Have you ever had to kill a man, Colonel?

Hamilton Me? No, I . . .

Arnold smiles, leans over and hits Hamilton on the thigh, and sits back.

Peggy What has my husband been accused of, Colonel Hamilton?

Hamilton hesitates, he wants to be sure that Arnold has no more to say, then:

Hamilton The first charge concerns the vessel, *Charming Nancy*. It is claimed that you granted persons of disaffected character passes. Which enabled them to transport this ship out of British-occupied Philadelphia, permitting a profit for these people.

Beat.

Arnold They asked for a pass. To sneak a ship away from our enemies. What is wrong with that?

Hamilton Their purpose was personal profit, sir.

Arnold How did I know that? Were their profits the King's profits? No. So what? Besides I did not know these men. I did not know their plans. Perhaps I erred in judgement. Why is that a crime?

Beat.

Hamilton Mr Reed believes you had a financial interest in the *Charming Nancy*. Thus – you would be working for your own gain. Using your position – for personal profit. (*Beat.*) Reed has no proof. I can tell you this. But I have to ask you: Do you or did you have an interest in this vessel?

Arnold The *Charming Nancy*?

Hamilton Yes.

Arnold Reed accuses me with no proof? (*He covers his face and shakes his head – to show the burdens he must bear.*)

Hamilton I take that to mean – no. (*As he writes.*) Excuse me.

Arnold turns to Peggy.

Arnold Schyler's his new father-in-law.

She nods, she knows this.

(*He turns to Hamilton.*) I was *his* aide-de-camp, you know. As you are to –

Hamilton (*writing*) I know.

Arnold (*looks to Hamilton, then to the women*) When Schyler was interviewing me for the position, he put his big bear-like hand on my shoulder, and pointed about a hundred yards across a field to a big bright red barn. 'Soldier!' he said in that warm voice he has.

This makes Hamilton smile, knowing how his father-in-law sounds.

'What colour is that barn?' I look at the barn. I look at your father-in-law's face. I look back at the barn. 'Any colour you wish it to be, sir!' (*He bursts out laughing.*) I was hired on the spot.

Hamilton can't help but laugh a little as well, though he continues to write.

Not an easy job, aide-de-camp. Not what people think. Is it?

Hamilton slightly shakes his head. Arnold sits back.

Good man, Schyler. A goddamn crime what the politicians did to him.

Hamilton (*still writing*) He seems to bear no bitterness.

Arnold Get him drunk.

Short pause.

Hamilton Second charge by –

Peggy (*interrupting*) Would you like more tea?

Hamilton (*shakes his head*) Second charge by Reed. Mr Reed. That as you closed the shops in Philadelphia under martial law, as was your right and responsibility –

Arnold And my orders.

Hamilton Yes, that you continued to personally trade the goods of said shops – for profit, as well as committing extortion against those businesses you did close. Profiteering, I have been asked to tell you, has become a crime promoted by Congress to a penalty of death.

Short pause.

Arnold Good. Start with the fucking politicians. Hang 'em all, would be a good start. Reed first. The man was a failed shopkeeper before this war began. Did you know that? And he's a rich man now. How did that happen?

Turns to Peggy as he shakes his head in disgust. She holds his hand.

Hamilton If you could answer the charge –

Arnold I was rich and now I've nothing. Nothing –

20

material. (*He strokes Peggy's arm. To Hamilton*) When do I get to ask where my back pay and premiums are? I have detailed to the Congress what this great patriotic duty has cost me – I have lost ships, lands, my home. I am owed two thousand in pay. I have personally paid for blankets in Maine out of my own accounts.

Hamilton Send receipts.

Arnold I've sent in the goddamn receipts! I have gained nothing from this war. It has taken my health. My fortune. I have made nothing. (*He sits back, suddenly tired, or he wants to show that he is tired.*) Pay me only what I'm owed, and let me go. I've had enough of this war. I have no more to give.

Hamilton You are a prized general in our Army, sir. You must know the respect each soldier feels for you. And the honour all those feel for having served alongside you.

Arnold stares at Hamilton, then turns to Peggy.

Arnold (*suddenly smiling*) Hear that? (*He shakes his head, then on to another story.*) When those of us stupid enough to survive fell out of the great northern woods and onto the banks of the St Lawrence – what we must have looked like. Half had no clothes. Their dicks frozen against their thighs. Keep walking, I said to them. Don't fight back. Don't question. We're good men. Fight a good fight. (*Beat.*) I love my country, Colonel Hamilton.

Hamilton I didn't –

Arnold (*over this*) The country I knew – is in here. (*Touches his breast.*) That helps – when I don't see it out there.

Short pause. Hamilton writes.
    Again geese are heard overhead. Arnold struggles and stands – refusing help from Peggy. And with an

imaginary rifle in hand, he pretends to shoot down a goose.

I hate cities.

Hamilton (*finishes writing*) Third charge.

Arnold (*interrupting*) I like this boy. He does his job.

Hamilton Third –

Arnold One minute. (*He struggles, perhaps too hard, to get back into his seat. Then he sits, leans over, and 'gives all of his attention' to Hamilton.*)

Hamilton Third – charge. You've been accused of illegally using – commandeering – public wagons for personal business ventures. I believe there was a vessel you did have an interest in. We have those papers. And goods from this vessel were transported by public wagons? You've heard the charge before? Is this true?

Arnold Yes.

Short pause.

Hamilton Is there anything you wish to add? An explanation?

Arnold picks up his cup, and Hannah pours him more coffee. When she finishes:

Arnold It is nowhere forbidden – to my knowledge – for one to engage in making money. The ship you refer to is – one such enterprise. (*He sets the cup down and with much less effort stands and limps as he continues.*) The goods transported from this vessel were goods – clothes, blankets, hides – much in need by our countrymen.

Peggy (*to Hamilton*) People are going cold –

Arnold (*over this*) And in transporting such goods I used public wagons which were not commandeered as you call it, but rather, sitting idle. And if you speak with the captain of these wagons – I'll give you his name – you will learn that I offered to pay for their use. A price determined not by me, but by the marketplace. What have I done wrong? (*Beat.*) Colonel, what have I done that was wrong?

Hamilton (*writing*) I cannot answer –

Arnold When this country needed me, I was one of the first to give up all. Where were they? Where were my accusers? (*Beat.*) But we are being naive. This – these attacks are not about me. The question is not what I have done wrong.

Hamilton What are you –?

Arnold I'll tell you, son – I'm but a pawn in this. A piece on the board to knock over, to get to their catch – your general, sir, our Commander-in-Chief, General Washington!

Hamilton I'm not sure that's –

Arnold They wish to replace him. Defeat him. They are afraid of his authority. They have Gates waiting in the wings. Someone they control –

Hamilton (*stops writing*) I won't take this down.

Arnold It's what this is about, boy! Open your eyes!

Hamilton (*over this*) You can't prove –

Arnold Don't you get it?

Peggy gets up and takes Arnold's hand. He calms down.

They are vile.

Hamilton (*to Hannah*) I'll have some more of that tea, thank you.

Hannah It's cold.

Hamilton I'm thirsty, please.

She pours him more tea. Peggy has taken a handkerchief out of her husband's pocket and now wipes his face. Hamilton takes a deep breath, turns a page in his book, and before continuing, he looks at Peggy.

Arnold What next? (*Realizes.*) My wife?

Hamilton A question. Not a specific accusation –

Arnold Because her father tried to choose the safety of his family over either side in this war? There is no shame in that! He's not a Loyalist! He's a husband and father!

Hamilton (*for the first time, stating his own opinion*) I don't agree with . . . (*Indicates the charge on the paper he holds.*)

Arnold (*over this*) And because my wife – (*Takes her hand.*) – during the occupation happened to dance a few times with British soldiers? She told me about this! So she danced! She is a girl! Look at her! She meant no politics!

Hamilton I agree, sir. I do agree with you on this –

Arnold (*over this*) She meant to dance! Would your wife have been any different?

Hamilton Probably not –

Arnold (*over this*) I have not gone to war against seventeen-year-old girls!

Hamilton Neither have I.

Arnold (*over this*) Is it now a crime to wear an English dress? To listen to English music? Goddamnit, son – we speak English! For this I watched men die? For this I killed? For this I gave my leg?

24

Hamilton (*at the same time*) No, no. No, sir.

Arnold If my marriage is my crime, then I am an unrepentant criminal!

Hamilton It isn't, sir.

Arnold (*over this*) Hang me, because I have a wife with taste! And grace! And beauty!

Hamilton I can assure you, it isn't a crime. Please.

Arnold (*over this*) So hang me! Hang me, soldier! Hang me!

Beat. They look at each other.

Hamilton As I said, I can see no crime there. Forgive me, but I have to repeat everything. You understand, I am sure.

Arnold slowly nods then suddenly slaps Hamilton on the back.

Arnold I don't blame you, son.

Hamilton Thank you.

Arnold You're a soldier. You do what you're told.

Hannah I'll get more tea. (*She stops, turns back. To Peggy*) The musicians are here.

Peggy Show them inside.

Hannah hurries off.

Will you stay the night, Colonel?

Hamilton I've promised friends –

Peggy Then at least for dinner. (*She starts to go in.*) They play as you eat. It helps the digestion. It's what they do in England. (*She follows Hannah in.*)

Hamilton There are seven more charges, sir. Bear with me. We'll get through them quickly, I'm sure.

SCENE FOUR

The same, later that night. Inside the house, the musicians play. Arnold sits alone, his leg propped up on another chair; he smokes a pipe. After a moment, Hannah enters from the house, feigns a look at the night sky, then:

Hannah They're dancing.

No response.

He's quite good. Polished. So is she. I hadn't seen Peggy dance before. She obviously enjoys it. Can I get you anything?

He shakes his head without looking at her.

They make quite a couple.

He looks at her.

Dancing. Ah – youth.

Arnold I'm not that old.

Hannah I am. And I'm three years younger than you. (*She leans over conspiratorially.*) He already has a crush on her. I suppose your wife does that with men. (*He tries to ignore her.*) And he's just married himself. Can't be more than a month, is it? I think that's what he said. His wife is rich?

Hamilton (*puffs on his pipe*) Yes.

Hannah So he's made a good match. (*Beat.*) You know he was born a bastard.

Arnold (*turning to her*) How would you know that –?

Hannah (*turning away*) The music's stopped. They've stopped. (*She listens.*) I never danced like that when I was young. When I was – no more than a child. Sometimes she looks no more than –

26

Arnold Hannah.

Hannah She took Mr Hamilton on a tour of the house.

Arnold Good.

Hannah She made it clear I wasn't to join them. Just her and him. They were gone about twenty minutes. (*Beat.*) She's had three glasses of wine.

Arnold Hannah, what are you now, a spy? Please let –

Hannah (*standing*) If I'm in the way –

Arnold I didn't mean –

Hannah (*over this*) I worry about you, maybe I'm the only one who does. (*She turns to leave.*)

Arnold I'm joking, come here! Sister, please! Come here.

Hannah stops, hesitates, then goes and takes Arnold's outstretched hand.

I appreciate . . . Everything. You must know that. (*He reaches up and hugs her, kissing her on the forehead. She nearly melts.*) What would I ever do without you.

Hannah (*over this*) You don't have to say –

Arnold I mean it!

Peggy and Hamilton burst in from the house.

Peggy (*entering, heading for Arnold*) Hannah, could you hand me that cushion? (*She goes and sits at Arnold's feet.*)

Arnold Please, sit – there's a chair –

Peggy I wish to sit here.

Hannah hesitates, then gets the cushion and hands it to Peggy. During this:

Hamilton I have to say, General, you are a most lucky

man. Your wife's beauty and charm surpass even her reputation.

Peggy (*to Arnold*) I thought he was a soldier, not a politician.

They smile.

Hannah (*giving Peggy the cushion*) What reputation is that?

Arnold (*to Peggy*) I think he's just an honest man.

Hamilton I was warned by General Washington to be on guard, or I'd be swept off my feet by your wife. I will report that I have failed him.

Light laughter.

Hannah Just don't report it to your new wife.

Beat. Then they laugh at the 'joke'.

Arnold He doesn't have a drink. We should get him a –

Hamilton (*over this*) I've had more than enough. More than I should, thank you.

Peggy (*over this*) Hannah, could you get the Colonel a –

Hamilton I have to leave. I do.

Beat.

Arnold I won't hear of –

Hamilton I must. (*Beat.*) Please, don't make it any harder than it is. (*He shakes his head to sober up.*) My wife has relatives in Philadelphia. They expect me. (*He looks at his watch.*) My God – they've been expecting me. The new in-laws. I wouldn't wish to inconven– (*He has trouble saying the word, then tries again.*) – inconvenience them. Somehow I've gotten a little drunk. (*He wipes his face.*)

Arnold That was our intention.

Hamilton, confused for a moment, looks at Arnold. Peggy suddenly laughs and slaps Arnold's arm.

Peggy Benedict!

Arnold The cool air will clear your head. It's too stuffy inside.

Hamilton nods, hesitates, then:

Hamilton I hope you're feeling better. (*He nods towards Arnold's raised leg.*)

Arnold I shouldn't have had the wine. I never learn.

Hamilton nods. He watches Arnold. Beat.

Is there anything . . .?

Hamilton I hope this afternoon was not too – painful. One does what one must.

Arnold I understand. Remember, I was secretary to your father-in-law.

This makes Hamilton laugh.

Hamilton I really must . . .

Arnold Hannah will show you out. Goodnight.

Peggy, still at Arnold's feet, holds up her hand. Hamilton shakes it.

Hamilton Good night. (*Then, staring at Arnold, blurting out.*) I much admire you, sir. (*He turns and hurries out with Hannah.*)

Short pause.
From the house, the musicians begin another tune, but soon stop.

Peggy (*listening*) They don't know whether to play or not. There's no one in there.

Arnold What did you find out? Anything?

Peggy (*her head on his thigh*) That General Washington has sided with you from the beginning. He's never believed the charges.

Arnold sits back and closes his eyes. Hannah returns carrying a small tray of glasses and liquor.

The fact that he has agreed to decide the matter personally is a very good thing. He knows what you've been going through. Such charges are even being circulated against him. They're being made against military governors in the south as well. (*Beat.*) You are supported. These depositions – a formality.

Arnold Then why put us through –?

Peggy They have no choice, he said. That boy is full of apologies.

Hannah sets the tray down.

Hannah Can you trust what he says? Are we sure –

Peggy (*ignoring her*) And I'm sure he wished you to know all this. He just couldn't tell you himself, of course.

Arnold So my responses this afternoon –

Peggy More than enough to address the charges. His recommendation to the General will be for complete exoneration. A recommendation the General shall accept with pleasure.

Arnold (*relieved*) Oh God.

Peggy (*to Hannah*) He told me all this while I showed him the house. You weren't there, were you?

Arnold The nightmare of my life may be over. My honour, my self-respect – survives. I am an honest man. And I am a damn good soldier. (*He hugs Peggy, and nearly weeps with joy.*)

Peggy He indicated that a request made now to return to a field command would be met with approval. They need you, Benedict.

Arnold It's where I can do some good.

He sits back. Hannah begins to pour him a drink.

No, I mustn't drink. I mustn't.

Peggy Hannah, take away the tray. What could you be thinking?

Hannah He always used to enjoy a drink before bed. I always got him a drink.

Peggy (*over this*) He can't any more, Hannah. It inflames his leg.

Arnold (*over this, reaching for the glass*) A little drink. A small one. It's been a good night. (*He takes a glass and sips.*)

Pause. Hannah sits and watches her brother. Both women now staring at this man.

(*He sips and stares out.*) At Saratoga, Gates ordered me away from the lines. He took away my men. My horse. (*He looks at them.*) I've told you this a hundred times.

Both women shake their heads. 'No, no, please.' 'Tell me.'

He'd taken everything from me – but my soul. I stole a horse. Disobeyed Gates. Charged to the line and led a charge that got so close to Bourgoyne I could see the blood rush out of his face. The powder off his wig on his shoulder.

I just remembered that. Seven bullet holes in my hat, my coat. Fate protected me. As it protects me now. Damn it, I'm a soldier and General Washington understands that. (*Beat.*) He understands me. A good man. If it weren't for him . . . Like a father to me. (*Beat.*) They say I looked crazed, deranged as I charged. And that really scared them. Good. You have to do what you have to do. You pull it out of you from somewhere. (*Beat.*) I gave my leg to my country. Now let me give it my life, if it wants it. Let me.

Peggy (*hugging Arnold*) I love you. It's a love greater than any I ever imagined possible. (*Beat.*) My love for you grows greater and stronger each day, each hour and each minute. (*She turns to Hannah.*) Like our baby.

She touches her stomach. He kisses her head.

Arnold (*to Hannah*) Sister, would you please pay the musicians. It's late and there's no one dancing.

Hannah goes off. Arnold helps Peggy up and she sits on his lap.

Peggy (*as she sits*) It doesn't hurt?

He kisses her. She sits back, and he takes out a letter and shows her.

Arnold Another from Andre. Or as he calls himself John Anderson. John Andre – John Anderson. He calls that a code. (*He smiles.*)

Peggy I warned you he wasn't very bright. When he was here – he spent all of his time acting, putting on plays –

She stops, he has put the letter up to the candle flame.

Arnold Patience. A virtue I have long sought – without success. I should have just waited. I should never have written. (*Holding up the letter.*) Do you mind? Will you be disappointed?

She shakes her head, and he burns the letter.

Peggy I don't care where I live as long as it's with you. (*She hugs him. Then touches her stomach.*) We'll go anywhere with you. Follow you – wherever. When I wake up, the first thought I have every day is that I am your wife, carrying your child. And I am so happy. I ask myself – what did I do to deserve such happiness?

They kiss.

If it's a boy, let's name him after the General, and call him George.

SCENE FIVE

New York City. A makeshift dressing room, backstage of the Theatre Royal, John St. In the distance, a performance of Richard III *is going on.*
    A British Officer, Lieutenant-Colonel John Simcoe, stands waiting, a file of papers to be signed in his hand.
    A noise off, he turns. Major Kemble enters, also with papers. They nod to each other, and wait. The performance continues off.

Kemble (*finally*) You're waiting for Sir Henry as well.

Simcoe I have papers for him to see.

Kemble shows his papers – he has papers for Sir Henry as well.

You knew where to find him.

Kemble Who doesn't?

Applause from the theatre.

Simcoe Major Andre's in this, isn't he?

Kemble I believe so. A small role.

Simcoe Is he as – talented – as they say?

Kemble I wouldn't know.

> *Andre, in costume* (*he plays a minor role in* Richard III), *enters with Sir Henry Clinton, who is in full uniform.*

Sir Henry (*entering*) I don't understand.

Andre You wanted to know who is sitting with Colonel Harvey, correct?

> *They notice Simcoe and Kemble. Andre goes to a table and sits and powders himself.*

I'm telling you, Sir Henry, she is Delancy's wife.

Sir Henry (*caught up in the gossip*) But then where's Delancy?

Andre He's – well, what I've been told is – in essence – he's rented her to Colonel Harvey.

Sir Henry I truly don't understand. You can't mean –

Andre Yes! We buy – the Army buys produce from Delancy. Harvey arranged this. So that's what Delancy gets. He's getting rich.

Sir Henry Unbelievable. (*to Simcoe and Kemble*) I can't fathom – (*He turns back to Andre.*) Off his wife's hole? (*He stands incredulous. Then, seeing the papers*) Are those for me? (*He takes them and skims.*)

Andre Would you like to meet her? She'd probably like to meet you.

Sir Henry I don't think – (*He turns to Kemble and laughs.*) No, I don't think I would at all. Can you believe that? The man rents his wife. Americans! I don't know why I let them surprise me any more! Are you watching?

John's terribly good tonight. Let me do that. You've missed a whole spot.

Sir Henry goes and powders Andre. Kemble stands and watches.

Kemble I'm sure the Major is a very fine actor. (*Beat.*) The theatre's not my pleasure, I'm afraid.

Sir Henry Neither was it mine until I saw John.

Simcoe (*going through his papers*) If that will be all?

Andre has unbuttoned his tunic.

Andre I'm sweating through this.

Sir Henry Let me. (*He begins to powder Andre's bare chest.*)

Simcoe looks at Kemble and leaves. Kemble hesitates, then turns back.

Kemble Oh Major – any reply from 'Monk'?

Beat. Andre looks at Sir Henry, then responds.

Andre Not yet. I expect – any time now.

Kemble I'm sure – you're in control of things.

Sir Henry We need patience. We just need to wait. John understands that.

Kemble goes, as the Stage Manager enters.

Stage Manager Your cue is coming, Major. (*Leaves.*)

Andre Thank you, Sir Henry. That will do fine. It's only a minor role. (*He laughs lightly and begins to exit.*)

Sir Henry I'll come and watch again from the wings. If that's all right. I enjoy that terribly.

They go.

35

*Morristown, New Jersey. Washington's headquarters. A
private room at Dickerson's Tavern. A small table and a
few chairs.*

  *Empty. Arnold, in full dress, walks in. He looks around.
Hamilton enters from another door.*

Hamilton General Arnold. I just heard you'd arrived.
You're a few minutes early. His Excellency will be with
you shortly.

Arnold Tell him to take his time. (*He smiles.*) I'm in no
rush.

  Hamilton sets a folder on the table.

How are you, Colonel? And how's your bride?

Hamilton I've hardly seen her for two months, sir. Would
you like something to drink?

  Arnold shrugs.

I'll get something for you. His Excellency isn't drinking.

Arnold Then don't bother, I won't –

Hamilton (*leaving*) He'll insist.

  *After a beat, General George Washington, 47, enters.
He looks exhausted. When he sees Arnold he lights up.*

Washington My God – it's a soldier! How the hell did you
get past all those politicians?

  Arnold smiles.

Arnold Just pushed my way through, sir. Shot a few along
the way. I hope you don't mind.

Washington Here – take a medal.

Hamilton enters.

Hamilton Are we feeding them or not?

Arnold doesn't know what he's talking about.

Washington (*to Hamilton*) No one offered to pay?

Hamilton shakes his head.

Unbelievable.

Arnold (*to Hamilton*) What's –?

Hamilton A delegation from Congress. I've put them in the next room.

Arnold And they expect the Army to feed them –?

Washington (*over this*) There's one a week now. Except when it rains.

Hamilton Or cold.

Washington I can't wait for winter. They leave you alone then.

Hamilton They've ordered food.

Washington Get the tavern keep to write out a bill. Put it in front of them. Point. These are not poor men.

Hamilton goes. Washington's mind drifts for a moment, then:

Mr Arnold, it is very good to see you. I ordered us lunch. You want to drink something –?

Arnold Colonel Hamilton –

Washington He won't bring the wine. He's hoarding the wine. It'll be rum.

Arnold I don't mind.

Washington In Philadelphia is there wine?

Arnold It can be found.

Washington They say you live well in Philadelphia.

Arnold In general? Or me personally?

Washington You, sir. What I've heard is about you.

Beat.

Arnold I am the Military Governor of the city. I am a general in the United States Army. I live no better nor worse than I must and should.

Beat.

Washington Why the hell didn't I say that? They were into my books just last month. Where's the receipt for this? Where's the receipt for that? I try to say when you lift a squealing pig off a Tory farm, it isn't too likely you'll get a receipt. What war are they fighting? I don't know. (*Beat.*) You must feel the same way.

Arnold Yes sir, I do.

Washington They want your scalp. (*Beat.*) And they want mine.

Arnold Do they?

Short pause.

Washington Well, this isn't about me, is it? Mr Adams has proposed in Congress that all generals should be elected. I wrote and said, great. I vote for Mr Adams to be on the front lines. (*Beat.*) He withdrew his proposal. They don't know what they are doing. And they're bringing us all down with them. Tell me what is the currency rate on the street? No one will tell me.

Beat.

Arnold I believe it's 500 US paper dollars to one guinea. But that was yesterday, it's probably worse now.

Pause.

Washington I tell them, get someone else. I'm not a military genius. Get Gates. He wants it bad. Look what he did to Schyler. Just because the man disagreed with him. No one wants to discuss anything any more. Everyone's screaming at everyone. Who's the real American? And they're all just such goddamn hypocrites! Your Mr Reed, your accuser – he's trying to bring God into this now. What the hell does God have to do with a war? If he'd been with us this winter – he'd have had to conclude that if he wanted to be on God's side, it wasn't ours. (*Short pause.*) There was a moment last winter – Hamilton knocked on my cabin. Twenty men – enlisted, wanted to see me. More desertion. More failure. They come in. I just look into the fire, waiting for them to begin to justify – Their families. Their farms. They're hungry. Who gives a shit, they're soldiers! But . . . (*He shrugs.*) Then, one begins to speak, a young boy really – how they have come to enlist again – for another year. In the midst of a blizzard. They had no shoes, Benedict. I looked at them. In the firelight. Their eyes red from sickness. Their clothes torn and bloody. And I went to each one . . . (*He begins to cry.*) And I hugged them. I held them. I told them how proud of them I . . . (*He can't go on for a moment.*)

> *Hamilton comes in with rum, glasses and food. As he sets these down on the table, he and Arnold exchange glances.*
> *Washington wipes the tears, pours himself a glass of rum.*

Rum. What did I tell you? (*He drinks.*)

> *Hamilton sits down at a distance.*

Are you broke too?

Short pause.

Arnold I can't sell my house in New Haven.

Washington Who'd buy it? And for what – our worthless paper money? I've started to burn it for heat. Wipe myself with it. Sometimes you feel like an utter fool. Everyone's getting rich. Everyone I know it seems.

Hamilton stirs in his chair.

Is that what this was really about – money? (*Beat.*) Makes you want to curse – the whole species, Mr Arnold. It can't just be an American trait, Benedict. It must be everyone. Somehow that gives some comfort.

Hamilton comes over and cuts the meat for Washington.

(*in pain, with his eyes closed*) Dr Rush has written an anonymous letter to Patrick Henry, calling me incompetent. (*Beat.*) Anonymous. I recognized the handwriting. I have spies too. (*Beat.*) Dr Rush is a very good and close friend of mine. (*Short pause. He drinks, turns to Hamilton.*)

Hamilton The delegation will see you whenever you're ready.

Washington (*to Arnold*) How's your beautiful young wife?

Arnold She's –

Washington I hear she's pregnant. Good for you. Have children, then you don't have to feel you must do everything yourself. In your life. A man's greatest mistake – not to have a child. I speak from experience. (*Beat. He suddenly smiles.*) Also a damn good excuse to make

40

yourself a little money – 'for the family'. Who argues with that?

Washington is more and more into himself. Arnold sits and watches this man who is in so much pain.

Do you dream, sir?

Arnold I do. But I can never recall what I've dreamed.

A knock on the door (off). *Hamilton gets up and goes to the door* (off), *exiting.*

Washington (*as he picks at his food*) Martha tells me I sit up and scream in the night. I don't recall either. I just remember how painful it was. I try to avoid sleep now. But that's not good, is it? God knows when I've slept last. (*Beat.*) They say we must end the war by next summer. (*Beat.*) Impossible. (*Beat.*) But then we run out of money. Bullshit. (*Pause.*) It is good to talk to a soldier.

Hamilton returns.

Hamilton They'd like to see you now.

Washington They'd like to see me. (*He pours himself more rum. To Arnold*) About a month ago, I was offered an Earldom. From the King. What do they take me for? They were going to throw in – the name of a city. My name. Washington. The name of a city. My choice. Philadelphia? Even Boston. I said who the hell wants a city named after him? They don't understand. Sometimes, I fear in my deepest soul, that no one understands. That I'm fighting this goddamn war for reasons that are perverse and contradictory. That I'm a pawn for speculators, embezzlers, stockjobbers, and a whole sea of monstrous intentions. But in my soul, we fight for principle. Or am I alone? (*Beat.*) Do you ever feel like that, Benedict?

No response.

Look what they've given me to get you to sign. Why no one else would do it, I don't know. There. (*He hands him a piece of paper.*) It's a loyalty oath. We're all signing them now. I signed mine last week. Ask me how humiliated *I* felt.

Arnold Why a loyalty –?

Washington Because they don't have anything else to think about! And they sit in their mansions, refusing to pay money for this war, and wonder why the hell does a man like Washington put up with us at all? Someday it's going to dawn on him just what a sucker he's been, so we better get him to sign a loyalty oath. So I signed. So sign. (*Beat.*) Sign.

Arnold hesitates, then signs his name. Hamilton takes the oath away. Pause; Washington looks into Arnold's face.

Hamilton Sir, they're waiting.

Washington (*to Arnold*) Do you believe in God, Benedict?

Arnold (*stunned by the question*) I – I don't know what to – I pray –!

Washington (*over this*) I don't mean a GOOD God, or even one with a HEAVEN where nice folk go, or to the DEVIL where the bad go. I'm not saying any particular kind of God. Just – God. (*Beat.*) Knowable or unknowable. Is there a God? Mr Hamilton thinks there isn't.

Arnold looks to Hamilton.

And he has just about convinced me.

Washington stands, as does Arnold. Washington opens the folder and takes out a paper.

Now, my apologies for this formality, but it's what I agreed to do. Let me read to you my rebuke.

Arnold Your what? I'm sorry?

Washington I've had to find you guilty of two of the charges.

Arnold is in shock.

(*He reads.*) 'The Commander-in-Chief would have been much happier in an occasion of bestowing commendations on an officer who has rendered such distinguished services to his country as Major General Arnold; but in the present case, a sense of duty and a regard to candour oblige him to declare that he considers his conduct in the instance of the permit as peculiarly reprehensible, both in civil and military views, and in the affair of the wagons as imprudent and improper.' (*He closes the folder.*) There. That's done. I hope they do replace me with Gates. Let's see him deal with this crap.

Arnold I don't understand, Your Excellency. I'm innocent.

Washington No doubt.

Arnold, confused, to each man.

Arnold I've done nothing wrong.

Washington looks away, Hamilton steps forward.

Hamilton The Committee of Pennsylvania threatened to withdraw support – wagons, supplies, from the Army unless you were punished. We had no choice.

Arnold That's bullshit! This is my honour!

Hamilton You're the butt of gossip. Of talk. You've lost the confidence of the people of Philadelphia. (*He tries to hand Arnold a piece of paper – his orders.*) You're relieved of your duty as Governor there. We understand you'd be interested in a field commission. Or command of a fleet?

Washington (*half to himself*) What fleet? (*He laughs.*)

Hamilton And can you ride a horse yet? (*Beat.*) We are assigning you to command the fort at West Point.

Washington It's a mess. You fix it.

Hamilton Sir, you have the appearance of scandal around you. We had no choice.

Arnold Cowards.

Hamilton (*getting upset*) You don't speak to His Excellency like that −!

Washington (*over this*) We compromised. They wanted you in jail.

Arnold It's not me they want. You know that yourself −

Washington Of course not.

Hamilton But we couldn't let them get to the General could we?

Washington I will make this up to you. You have my promise.

He holds out his hand. Arnold doesn't take it.

Arnold You betrayed me.

Washington That's one opinion. Mine is that outside this tavern are twelve thousand men waiting for blankets, food, pay. It's them I must not betray. (*Beat.*) You are acting far too upset. It's a piece of paper. You still have my confidence.

Arnold Then say that! Write that down!

Hamilton He can't.

Arnold (*over this*) Just tell that delegation!

*Washington holds out his hands – gesturing there is
nothing he can do. Arnold bolts away from the table.*

Washington (*to Hamilton*) Let the bastards wait. That's
what I do every day. Maybe one of them will get the hint
and pay their bill. (*He tries to smile.*) General, sit down
and have another drink.

Washington pours. Arnold stays at a distance.

How's the wife? A beautiful woman, isn't she, Colonel?

Hamilton I'm in love with her myself.

Washington (*pouring, to Hamilton*) You told me you
danced with her?

Hamilton (*accepting a glass*) The high point of my visit to
Philadelphia.

Washington (*drinking*) He's a lucky man. (*Beat.*) And
she's expecting. Good for you. (*He turns to Hamilton.*)
How come yours isn't pregnant yet?

Hamilton Sir, I've hardly been allowed home since –

Washington (*winking at Arnold and laughing*) Excuses!
The boy makes excuses! I wouldn't! (*He laughs.*) But these
young ones . . . Look at him, Benedict. (*He 'presents'
Hamilton to Arnold.*) He still thinks the world will wait
for him.

*Washington smiles at Arnold, then patronizingly takes
Hamilton's hand and pats it.*

Well, son, it won't. (*He puts down his glass and
straightens his coat.*) I suppose I've put it off as long as I
can. Politicians. (*He shakes his head. He looks at Arnold
who stares at him.*) My regards, General, to your beautiful
young wife.

Washington goes. Short pause.

Hamilton Don't do anything you'll regret. (*Beat.*) He loves us like sons. So think of his pain. Accept West Point. There are worse places. (*He turns to go, stops.*) There's a guard posted outside their room. (*He nods towards where Washington exited.*) When His Excellency meets with members of Congress, they don't wish to be disturbed. (*Beat.*) Go home. Your horse is outside. Saddled.

Arnold I didn't ask –

Hamilton I did. I thought you'd wish to leave – quickly.

Hamilton leaves.

SCENE SEVEN

Philadelphia; the Penn Mansion, sitting room.
Arnold enters, his coat dusty from the road. (He has just arrived back from Morristown.) He begins to take off his coat. Hannah, in a nightgown, arrives, candle in hand.

Hannah What are you doing back? I thought you weren't coming home until –

Arnold (*still removing his coat*) Get me something to eat.

Hannah hesitates.

Please, Hannah. I haven't eaten.

Hannah hurries off. Arnold gets his coat off, and flings it on the ground. He throws himself into the chair and begins to try and take his boots off. This clearly is causing him both pain and frustration.
Hannah enters with a tray just as he finally gets a boot off and flings it across the room.

46

She goes and brings him the tray. He begins to eat. She watches.

Hannah You must be tired. It's so late. I couldn't sleep myself. (*She looks at him for a moment.*) I'm not sure this is the right time, but I would like to raise something with you. It's been on my mind all day. It's why I couldn't – sleep.

He eats.

While I was in one of the shops today, Mrs – you don't know her – a friend of mine, she asks how Peggy is doing.

Arnold looks up at her as he continues to eat.

I say, what do you mean? She – Peggy's – perfectly fine. And then she says, I mean with the pregnancy. It's often the first two months that are the most difficult. She says this as if I'd never heard it. As if I couldn't know. Well, Benedict, I was told by you – and Peggy – ordered – that this 'situation' – Peggy's, it was to be kept private. So I've said nothing. And there are many people I would have liked to have told. (*Beat.*) So is it private or not? I've told no one.

Arnold (*incredulous*) Hannah –

Hannah I will admit, Benedict, to feeling hurt. When I heard – it was like she thought *I* didn't know. You can imagine the position that puts me in –

Arnold suddenly can't take it any more, the frustration mounting from his talk with Washington erupts at Hannah.

Arnold Goddamnit woman, stop it! Will you be quiet! I can't take your stupidity any more! Stop! Stop!

Hannah bursts out crying, and moves away. Peggy enters in a nightgown.

Peggy What's –? Benedict, when did you –? Hannah?
What happened? Hannah?

*She goes to Hannah who pushes her away and runs out
of the room. Peggy looks at her husband. Pause.*
      Hannah can be heard crying – off.

Arnold I've been found guilty of two crimes. By General
Washington.

Peggy How can . . .? (*She stops herself.*)

Arnold And I've been censured. And sent away.

Peggy That's not possible.

Arnold It feels like they've rammed a hand down my
throat and reamed my soul.

Peggy There's been a mistake. You've misunderstood.

Arnold (*over this*) He traded me for wagons! (*He takes
out a very crumpled newspaper.*) His published verdict.

*Peggy takes it and begins to read. Hannah slowly
returns at a distance.*

Peggy (*as she reads*) I don't believe this.

*Hannah cautiously approaches with a letter in hand.
She sniffles hard, trying not to cry.*

Arnold Hannah, I didn't mean –

Hannah This just came.

He takes the letter.

Peggy At this hour?

Arnold tries to pull Hannah towards him.

Arnold Hannah . . . (*He tries to kiss her on the cheek.*) I
didn't mean – of course, it must have been awful for you,

48

hearing that woman talk about – our baby. (*The 'our' he makes clear refers to the three of them.*) But things get out. So forgive me. (*He turns back to Peggy.*) There's more: I've been made commander of the fort at West Point. On the Hudson.

Peggy Why would –?

Arnold I'm out of the way there, I suppose.

Hannah I don't think we should leave –

Arnold (*yells*) We have to! (*He then quickly grabs her hand, to keep her from crying.*) There is no choice.

Pause. Peggy finishes reading the verdict and sets it down.

(*to no one*) All the way back, I kept listing the battles I have fought in.

Peggy And I thought Washington was your –

Arnold He's not. (*Short pause.*) It's beautiful country. Around West Point. Dramatic. (*He smiles.*) Memorable. I was thinking, on our way up there, we could detour a little, reach the Hudson say at Tappan and follow the river from there? I wouldn't mind seeing it all again – one more time. As I remember it changes just about every mile.

Peggy You know it well then –?

Arnold I've been up and down that river more times than I can count.

Peggy goes and comforts Hannah. She hugs her.

First – at Haverstraw Bay – you'd think you were on the edge of a sea. It's vast, more lake than river, with green tumbling hills, dipping into the river's shore. As idyllic a picture as one can imagine, I would think. (*Beat.*) Then there's a sudden twist, and the river narrows ten times, and this lake becomes a twisting river of force, it cuts through mountains on one side, farms on the other. The wild west – divided from the settled earth. It's how it feels.

Hannah continues to cry.

And then another sudden turn, and it's a gorge you're in now. Steep slopes, cliffs, and there before you – on the west side, is West Point. With its forts, buildings, old walls, as but the foreground for the glorious Catskills behind. Huge peaks of nature, nature untouched by people – pristine, raw and free. Uncompromised earth. (*Beat.*) Were I to ever leave –

Peggy turns when she hears this.

– it is what I would miss of my country. Such beauty. Such places. (*Beat.*) You'll see. We'll detour.

Peggy moves from Hannah and approaches Arnold.

Peggy Were *we* to ever leave . . . (*She takes his hand, then looks off.*) Though sometimes it feels like we've already left. Or what we had – is gone. Last spring at the Meschianza Ball? I've told you about – by the way, that's where I first met John Andre.

He looks at her.

Remember him?

Hannah Who's John Andre?

Peggy The dress I wore was made of silk. A pale green and it flowed – like an animal running over a hill, that smoothly. The dressmaker was such a success. I'm told the style was the latest in London. I felt I was the belle of the ball.

Hannah Who's John –

Arnold A Major. British.

Hannah starts to say something, but Peggy interrupts.

Peggy (*to Arnold*) It was actually more than a ball. More like being inside a fairy tale. With knights and princesses. My friend Peggy Chew was saying the other day that she was dying to put on a play. Just for fun. What harm could that be? (*Beat.*) But plays are forbidden here. Why?

He looks at her, then turns away.

Arnold I don't know.

She waits to see if he has more to say, then continues.

Peggy In New York City they are still doing plays. Having concerts. *They* haven't closed anything. But then of course – that's the British influence. Culture. (*She remembers suddenly.*) My dressmaker for the ball? She's dead. Starved to death, I think.

Arnold has been fiddling with the letter in his hand. Peggy suddenly takes it, opens it and quickly reads the few lines.

From Reed. And the Committee. They've seen the verdict. (*She hands the letter back to her husband.*) We're to vacate this house by noon tomorrow.

Hannah Tomorrow? We can't possibly –!

Peggy (*over this, to Arnold*) We have to leave by tomorrow! He says you were fortunate to have got off so easy.

Arnold still doesn't look at the letter.

But he got what he wanted. (*to Hannah*) And we'll take only one trunk. And we'll carry it out the front door ourselves. Let them see how little we possess. What little he has left!

Short pause. They say nothing. The candle flickers, and

suddenly Peggy grabs her stomach, flinching.

Arnold (*taking her hand*) What? You feel the baby? Is it kicking?

Peggy (*shaking her head*) I think it's too soon for that. (*to Hannah*) Is it?

Hannah I don't know.

Short pause.

Peggy I saw a man on the street yesterday, who was getting money from people for farting in such a way that it almost sounded like 'God Save The King'. I couldn't watch. What a country. (*Beat. She rubs her stomach.*) Margaret Chew says that hundreds and hundreds of books – (*She takes Arnold's hand and rubs it across her stomach.*) – aren't even sent to America. Because nobody reads here.

Arnold (*pulling his hand back*) That isn't true!

She looks at him.

Peggy Hardly anyone.

Pause.

Arnold Maybe.

She takes his hand and holds it in hers.

Peggy Father says, nearly everyone's started going back to church. They feel they have to. He says, they're afraid if they're not seen in church things will be said about them. (*Beat.*) So loving your country isn't enough any more, Father says. Now you have to love your country's God. (*Beat.*) People are scared. They're afraid to say what they really think. That's what Father says.

Short pause.

*Months later. Haverstraw, five miles south of West Point.
A field overlooking the Hudson River. Night. Howling
wind.*

Andre (*off*) Mr Monk? Is that you?

Andre, out of uniform, enters, holding up a lantern.

Sir?

Arnold enters from the opposite direction. Short pause.

Arnold Mr – Anderson?

*They look at each other for a moment. Andre hears
something and turns to where Arnold entered.*

Andre Who's that?

Arnold My orderly. He'll keep his distance.

Andre Wouldn't it be best to . . .

Arnold (*turns, and calls*) Sergeant, stay with the horses!
(*back to Andre*) Why aren't you in uniform?

Andre (*ignoring him, looking off*) What a thrilling night.
Is it not? One could not imagine anything more dramatic.

Arnold It's an area I'm very fond of – the Hudson.

Andre I've journeyed up it myself. Soon after I arrived in
this country. To Quebec. To fight you, General.

Arnold looks at him.

I'm a great fan of yours. You've been quite the thorn in the
side. I admire that. Soldier to soldier.

Arnold (*looks towards the Hudson*) Your ship, *The
Vulture*, it's staying too close. My men will shell it. It
should move off and come back – for the pick up.

Andre Perhaps we should go now then. While it's there. You've brought nothing with you? (*Beat.*) Or are you still unsure?

Arnold (*suddenly*) How committed are you British to winning this war?

Andre Sir, I can promise –

Arnold (*over this*) Do you have the stomach for it? I have wondered that often enough. Your Army sits in New York –

Andre Sir Henry believes patience –

Arnold I need to know the depth of your passion! I need to know if you *believe*! And that you will act justly and honourably upon your beliefs! (*Beat.*) Have I made myself clear?

   Beat.

Andre I can assure you, sir, that as long as there's an England, these colonies will be *of* that England. You have my word. Sir Henry Clinton is as committed to this cause as he is to his own life. And I, sir, am willing to suffer a painful death for its noble sake.

   Short pause. Arnold says nothing.

Should we go?

   There is no response.

We haven't talked compensation.

   Arnold turns to hear this.

For such a brave act as this, my government expects to pay – something. Out of gratitude. Having you on our side will do much for morale, for one thing. What are you seeking?

Arnold (*after some hesitation*) I wish only to be given what I'm already owed by Congress both in back pay and loans made. (*Beat.*) And – for the value of my property in New Haven which shall surely be confiscated, when my actions here become known. (*He looks at Andre.*)

Andre Do you have a figure amount?

Arnold In pounds?

Andre What else is there?

Beat.

Arnold Ten thousand. And this constitutes no profit on my behalf. Only reimbursement –

Andre I understand –

Arnold And pay for what I'm giving up. My claim's now in –. I do not wish to end up indigent in my –

Andre I understand. And what you ask seems fair –

Arnold (*over this*) I am no Judas. This is not how I see myself, nor how I wish to be seen. I do not do this for money! It is my hope that my actions here will give courage to others to do the same. And if I accept no more than what I'm owed, then the virtue of what I do can't be questioned. It will be seen I act in good conscience, honour intact, and for what is in the best interest of my country.

Beat.

Andre I salute you. It is indeed a noble thing you do. I am in a position to guarantee the request.

Andre looks to Arnold, expecting him to go with him now, but Arnold hesitates, then sits on the ground.
Andre takes out a flask.

Would you like a . . .? (*He notices that this flask is nearly empty.*) I have another.

55

He takes out another, offers to Arnold, who ignores it.
Then Andre takes a big swig himself. In fact, it slowly
becomes clear that Andre is himself a bit drunk already.
Andre, to be friendly, sits on the ground as well.

(*after a pause*) Beautiful night. How is your lovely wife? I
assume she must be . . .? She'll be joining you, I assume.

Arnold She's fine. (*Beat. For a moment he is lost in
thought.*) She says you're a – poet?

Andre (*smiling*) I've written –

Arnold (*over this*) And actor. She talks about a ball, when
you were in Philadelphia.

Andre (*over this*) The Meschianza.

Arnold I can never understand what she's – it sounds so –
it doesn't make sense.

Andre (*over the end of this*) A little something to keep the
men's spirits up. A festival really. To celebrate General
Howe's return to London. (*Beat.*) I created a tilt and
tournament, like those of the ancient knights. We had
armour, I was in charge of the hats myself, I could step
into the life of a milliner now. Should one want that.
(*Beat.*) We had jousts. The ladies dressed in Turkish
costume. Your wife was adorable. It was fun. Everyone in
Philadelphia had fun. Everyone invited. It cost a fortune.
(*He laughs.*) It was like a play, but without an audience,
only actors. The Knights of the Blended Rose. Their
motto: 'We droop when separated.' (*He laughs and
drinks.*) The Knights of the Burning Mountain. Their
motto: 'I burn for ever.' (*He smiles.*) We redid a whole
mansion. You walk in and it's like – hundreds of years
ago. It got us through the winter. The General was very
pleased.

   Beat.

Arnold My wife had a good time.

Andre My greatest achievement in America – so far. It's why I'm a major. Caused a hell of a lot of resentment – my promotion. But this – (*gestures towards Arnold*) – will change everything for me. (*Beat.*) Sir, I think we should go.

Arnold I am not coming with you today, Major Andre.

Andre (*suddenly standing and angry*) Then what am I doing here? Why did you insist that I come? I do not enjoy wasting my time –

Arnold I asked you to come – (*He gets Andre's attention.*) – so that I could offer you not only myself, but my command, the three forts at West Point, and its three-thousand-eighty-six men. They are yours.

    Andre is stunned. After a pause.

Andre And how is such an offer – to be accepted? Will you march them down the river –

Arnold (*takes maps and papers out of his coat*) A tally of my army's strength, maps of the forts, with locations of weakness marked. A copy of the plan in event of alarm, again with weaknesses indicated. A proposed attack plan, including strength needed, types of equipment and so forth. You will see that as presently organized, West Point stands completely vulnerable, to even the most modest assault. And with myself in charge of the defenders, there can be no chance of failure. (*He holds out maps and papers to Andre.*) It's now clear why I insisted that we meet?

Andre (*walking around, excited*) My God, they'll make me a bloody general. And they laugh at me now. I know they do. (*to Arnold*) I came to this godforsaken country because – I was a bloody clerk at home. They wouldn't even let me become an actor! So I'm here. Two thousand men! (*He opens the flask. Offering*) Please . . .

Arnold I'm not finished. (*Beat.*) This assault must be taken tomorrow night. For good reason. This morning, in a few hours, a guest will arrive in my house. I shall spend the day with him, showing him the weakness of our fortifications. This will disappoint him, but not make him suspicious. As he visits in part to make amends for errors made towards me. (*Beat.*) I will forgive him. Embrace him. And he will spend the night. (*Beat.*) He is General George Washington. Commander-in-Chief of our Army. With the capture of West Point, you capture him. (*Beat.*) A good man. He's supported me throughout my political troubles, coming to my aid again and again. There have been times, when I saw him as my father. (*Short pause.*) You achieve this, Major, and the war is over.

> *Silence. The wind. Then birds are heard overhead. Arnold looks up.*

They should be asleep.

> *Cannon fire is heard off.*

Andre What's that?

Arnold My men are firing on your ship. You'd better signal to be picked up. I'll try to get them to stop.

> *More cannon fire. Andre takes a swig from his flask. Arnold watches where the cannon shot hits in the river.*

They're close. Your ship can't send a launch now.

Andre What am I going –?

Arnold (*over this*) I'll get a couple of men from the battery to row you over. I'll tell them – you're taking messages from me.

Andre takes another swig.

Just signal for them not to leave!

Andre General. You are the first true American patriot.

Arnold Don't kiss my ass, Major. I've never found that pleasant. And do stop drinking. (*He looks at him.*) My God, have I made a mistake?

Andre You haven't, sir. I give you my word. And I am sober. (*He takes the flask and throws it into the woods.*) Good day, sir. And good fortune.

Arnold Hide those papers. And signal!

> *Arnold hurries off.*
> *Cannon fire continues. Andre holds the papers, wonders where to hide them. He takes off his boot and stuffs them in. Then with the lantern he stands signalling the boat, using the lamp's shutter.*
> *More cannon fire; voices shouting are heard in the near distance. Andre hears them, turns to them.*

Andre Here! I'm here!

> *Two Skinners (half soldier/half highwayman) enter and stop when they see the smiling Andre.*
> *Andre turns and sees a signal from the ship.*

They'll stay where they are. But we should go. Where's the boat?

> *Beat.*

Pauling What boat?

Van Wart (*noticing*) They've stopped shelling. Why'd they do that? It's still in range. (*to Andre*) Who are you?

Andre Weren't you sent by General –

Pauling No one sent us.

Van Wart (*over this*) Who are you?

Andre (*realizing*) Oh God. Where's –? (*He looks for Arnold's men.*) My name is Anderson. John Anderson. Merchant. I have a pass. (*He begins to look in his jacket.*) From your commanding officer, General Arnold –

Van Wart We're local. Private soldiers.

Andre (*panicking*) I need to go, please.

They stop him.

My God, I must get along! I'm doing the General's business!

Pauling Look at them boots. Them are British soldier boots.

Andre I bought *them* in New York. That's all they sell. What do you want? I have a pass! (*He takes out a paper.*) Will you look at it?

Van Wart What are you doing out here at night?

Andre Damn it, man, will you listen to me! What do you want? You want to rob me? Here – it's all I have. (*He hands him his purse.*)

Van Wart British money.

Andre I live in New York! Of course I have – it's real money. If you want more – give me your names. I'll send some – or on my next trip to West Point –

Pauling Give me your boots. Look at my boots. I need boots.

Andre (*over this*) I can't give you my boots! What else? Here, take my cloak. It's wool.

Van Wart (*suddenly hits him across the face*) Give Mr Pauling your boots!

Andre falls down, bleeding from the mouth. Pauling takes off Andre's boots.

(*to Pauling*) Give me his cloak! I need his cloak!

Andre watches as Pauling finds the papers in the boot.

Pauling (*to Van Wart*) What's this?

Andre suddenly runs off in his bare feet.

Van Wart Hey, you bastard! Get back here! Get him!

The two Skinners run off in pursuit.
After a moment Arnold's two Soldiers enter with a lantern. They look around.

Soldier Mr Anderson? (*He calls.*) Mr Anderson?

They go off.

(*off*) Mr Anderson? Mr Anderson?

SCENE NINE

West Point. A room in Arnold's house overlooking the Hudson River. Table, a few chairs. Night.
Arnold enters, sweating and tired (he has just returned from his meeting with Andre). Hannah follows him, lighting a lamp. Arnold sits, then turns, hearing voices off.

Arnold Who's that? Peggy?

Hannah nods and sets the lamp on the table.

She's still up? (*He listens.*) Who's she with? Who's she talking to?

Hannah Colonel Hamilton. He arrived a few hours ago, to prepare for His Excellency's visit.

Short pause.

Arnold Tell my wife I'm here.

Hannah I wouldn't want to disturb them. They sound like they're – enjoying themselves.

Arnold (*over the end of this*) Tell her, Hannah.

> *Hannah goes off. Voices. Arnold takes out a pipe, and fills it. Peggy, very pregnant now, enters with Hamilton. Hannah follows. Peggy and Hamilton both carry glasses.*

Peggy You're back. (*She goes to kiss him.*)

Hamilton (*at the same time*) General, how are you?

Arnold (*at the same time, trying to stand*) Colonel, I didn't expect you tonight –

Hamilton (*over this*) Don't get up.

> *An awkward moment, no one knows what to say.*

(*finally*) Being in the country has done you a lot of good, sir. Your colour's back. You look so much more relaxed.

Arnold (*tense*) I am.

> *Short pause.*

Hamilton (*to say something*) You put in late hours. This was supposed to be an easy assignment.

Arnold The General's coming. I wanted everything ready for him.

Peggy And is everything ready?

Arnold Yes. I think so. I've done what I could.

Peggy Colonel Hamilton's been telling me all the gossip from Philadelphia.

Arnold You've been there?

Hamilton Passed through.

Peggy The new commander's already in trouble.

Arnold No doubt a crook – like me. (*Beat. He reaches for the bottle and pours into Hamilton's glass, and then his own.*) Tell me something – why take it?

Hamilton (*confused*) I don't understand. Take what?

Arnold Why does *he* take it? General Washington. The crap. The lies. They'd like to kill him you know.

Hamilton I don't think that's true –

Arnold (*over this*) They'd like him to fall off his goddamn horse and break his neck. How's that?

Hamilton That may be true for some.

Arnold And he knows this. (*He shakes his head and drinks.*) But then the *men* love him. He sees this. My men do. They're so excited about him arriving. Paying us the honour.

Hamilton He's come to pay honour to you. What happened in Morristown –

Arnold I forget everything. A soldier has to have a short memory, Colonel. If he didn't, after being in one battle, he'd never go into another. You haven't been in a battle yet, you haven't killed yet, have you?

Hamilton No.

Arnold Wait. (*He drinks.*) All is forgotten. (*Short pause.*) Loved, he is. The way they speak of him. To them, a god. We know better of course. (*He winks at Hamilton who doesn't smile.*) Oh come on – smile. You're not betraying the man by smiling. We know his faults. (*Beat.*) But they love him. The men. (*He drinks.*)

Hamilton Like they love you.

Arnold is taken aback by this.

I better go to bed. (*He starts to go.*)

Arnold Don't get me wrong. I love the General too. He's great. He's very very great.

Peggy I'll show you to your room.

Hamilton I think I can find –

Peggy (*over this*) Please. I'll take the light. (*She picks up the lantern.*)

Hamilton (*to Arnold*) Motherhood becomes her.

Peggy That is a great lie, Colonel. Motherhood becomes no one. I count the days until I've shed my burden.

They go.

Hannah I'll clean up. (*She picks up glasses, the bottle.*) The General will be here in the morning. That is exciting. You look tired. Another drink?

He nods. She pours. He drinks it all in one swallow. He stands, pushing back the chair. He sighs, exhausted; air just comes out of him, deflating him. He steadies himself as he begins to feel the drinks.

Arnold Tell Peggy – I went to bed.

He goes off. After a moment the Orderly enters. The room is nearly dark.

Orderly Is the General here?

Hannah He went to bed.

Orderly (*hesitates, then*) Could you tell him, we never found Mr Anderson.

Hannah (*repeating*) You never found Mr Anderson.

Orderly Yes.

Hannah I'll tell him. Goodnight.

Orderly Goodnight.

He goes. Peggy hurries across the room on her way to the bedroom.

Hannah The Orderly just said –

Peggy Sh-sh! We need to get to sleep. (*She rubs her face.*) Tomorrow's an important day.

She goes. Hannah takes the glasses and bottle off to the kitchen.

SCENE TEN

The same. Morning. A cock crows in the distance.
Arnold hurries in putting on his coat. Peggy, in her nightclothes and robe, runs in behind him. Hannah is alone at the table.

Arnold (*shouting*) Damn it, why wasn't I woken up? (*He goes to the door and screams to an Orderly.*) Tell His Excellency I'll be right there! I should be with him! (*He turns to Hannah.*) The General's arrived.

Hannah I know.

Arnold (*over this, not listening*) He's touring my forts! I look out my goddamn window and he's out there! Wake up Colonel Hamilton.

Hannah He's awake. And gone.

This stops Arnold and Peggy.

65

He's with His Excellency.

Beat.

Arnold Why wasn't I woken?

Hannah The Lieutenant said not to.

Arnold What Lieutenant?

Hannah The one who came to get the Colonel.

Arnold (*confused, he looks at Peggy then screams*)
Orderly! Orderly!

An Orderly hurries in.

He's arrived and no one told me. The General's out there
inspecting the fortifications without me. Why would he do
that?

The Orderly doesn't know.

(*calmer*) Mr Anderson, you got him back safely to his
ship, did you not?

The Orderly looks at Hannah.

Hannah (*trying to help*) No they –

Orderly We never found him, sir.

Arnold You never found him? You never found – Mr
Anderson?

Orderly No –

Arnold Jesus Christ! (*He screams.*) They never found him!

Hannah I was supposed to tell you, but Peggy said –

Arnold Be quiet. (*He sighs, tries to think what to do, takes
Peggy's hand.*) It'll be all right. It'll be all right.

Orderly Sir? A Mr Anderson, it's being said this morning,

66

has been captured in the village.

Arnold Captured? Why?

Orderly He's being held as a spy, sir. A British spy.

Peggy groans and nearly faints. Arnold grabs her.

Arnold (*to the others*) Help her to a seat. Get her to a seat!

Hannah (*over this*) What's –? I don't understand –?

A cannon is fired off.

Arnold That's the salute for His Excellency. He's arriving.
(*to Orderly*) Tell him, I'll be there – momentarily. Go! Go
greet His Excellency!

The Orderly, confused, hurries off.

Peggy (*nearly in shock*) Benedict, what's happened? (*She
tries to reach out to him; he is lost in thought.*)

Arnold (*half laughing*) Anderson. He was drunk.

Peggy Drunk? You didn't say –

Arnold (*over this*) The son of a bitch! They moored too
close! I gave it to them. They had it in their hands.

Peggy I haven't packed anything. I didn't dare.

Hannah What's –? I don't understand!

Arnold (*over this*) They could have captured Washington!

Hannah (*grabbing at Arnold*) Brother!

He pushes her away.

Arnold (*to Peggy*) Tell her.

Arnold moves away.

Peggy We have – changed sides, Hannah. In this war. We
now support the British.

Hannah The British?

Peggy (*over this*) It was the right thing to do! We had no choice. Your brother had suffered enough humiliation.

Arnold (*turning back to them*) That wasn't the reason, I wished to support –!

Peggy (*she tries to hold him*) I know! I know!

Hannah (*over this*) I know nothing of this! Why wasn't I told anything about this?

   Gunshots off. Beat.

Peggy What's . . .?

Arnold The final salutes. He's here. (*Beat. To himself*) Dear God, how did this happen? (*to Peggy*) He knows. That's why they didn't send for me. They've been – looking around, to see what I've done.

Peggy Then Andre's talked?

Hannah Who's Andre?

Arnold (*over this*) Or they found the maps. I gave him maps.

Peggy (*over the end of this*) You gave maps to a drunk! You stupid man!

Arnold He was your friend, not mine! (*He pushes Peggy away and immediately regrets it.*)

Peggy They'll hang us.

Hannah (*cries out*) Nooooo!

   More gunshots off.

Arnold My men know nothing. They wouldn't have been told. The British frigate's still in Haverstraw Bay. My men can row me there.

Peggy You mean us.

Arnold just looks at her.

You're not leaving me behind. I can't stay behind!

Arnold It's – the safest thing. If I'm caught . . . You – don't know anything, Peggy. You – don't – know – anything.

Peggy Don't leave me. Don't leave me. They'll kill me!

Arnold (*over this*) It's the right thing! Think of the child!

Peggy grabs him and starts hitting him, shouting 'No!'

(*to Hannah*) Take her! Take her! (*to Peggy*) They will not hurt you! (*He pushes her into Hannah's arms.*)

Hannah What about me?

Arnold (*ignoring her*) I'll go across the porch. They're out front now.

Peggy (*being held by Hannah*) You bastard! I hate you! I hate you!

She breaks free of Hannah and attacks Arnold. Their embrace quickly turns into a hug. He holds her against his chest. She cries.

Arnold (*holding her*) I'll send for you. It'll be fine. I cannot live without you. Please, Peggy.

A knock at the door.

Please, Hannah, take her. Hannah.

Hannah gently pulls Peggy off Arnold. And with only a quick glance back, he hurries off. Pause.
Another knock on the door.
Peggy slowly calms down. She takes long deep breaths.

Peggy (*finally, to Hannah, quietly*) Answer it. Answer it, or they'll be suspicious.

> *Hannah goes and answers the door. She returns with Colonel Hamilton.*
> *Peggy suddenly sits up, she smiles – she begins her 'performance'.*

Colonel Hamilton. I hear you were up quite early. I hope the bed was satisfactory.

Hamilton It was fine, ma'am.

Peggy But soldiers never sleep do they? I should know that by now. (*She smiles.*)

Hamilton Is your husband here? The General's anxious to speak with him.

Peggy My husband? He's – (*She shrugs. Then to Hannah*) Is he in his study? Hannah, see if he's in his study.

> *Hannah hesitates.*

Hannah, please. The Colonel's waiting.

> *Hannah goes off. Hamilton, anxious, sighs.*

Hamilton You are sure he is in the house?

Peggy Is something the matter, Colonel?

> *He turns and looks at her.*

Would you like some coffee –?

Hamilton Your husband has been defamed, Mrs Arnold.

Peggy Who by, this time? (*She smiles.*) I've had nothing to eat myself –

Hamilton (*interrupting*) Papers, plotting an assault from inside your husband's command, have been uncovered, ma'am. As well as a spy.

Peggy A spy? A real spy? How interesting for you.

Hamilton We've yet to speak with him ourselves. We've asked him to be brought here. I thought your husband should question him. Would you mind if I went upstairs to look?

Peggy Of course not.

Hannah returns.

Hannah He's not in his study.

This stops Hamilton, who is getting more and more concerned.

Peggy An assault from inside. I don't think I understand.

Hamilton Treason, Mrs Arnold. Are you positive he didn't leave the house?

Peggy Where would he be going? He is expecting the General. (*She turns to Hannah.*) Did you look in our bedroom?

A Soldier bursts in.

Soldier General Arnold's just been spotted in a batteau. Headed for the British frigate.

Hamilton (*suddenly turns*) Stop him!

Soldier I believe he's too far, sir.

Beat.

Hamilton Let the General know.

Soldier The General was one of those who spotted him, sir.

Short pause. Hamilton is in shock. Peggy watches him closely, then he suddenly turns on her.

Hamilton (*screaming*) You lied to me! You knew where he was!

Peggy (*frightened*) I knew nothing! What are you talking about? Hannah!

Hamilton (*over this*) God damn him! I believed him!

Hannah (*over this*) Leave her alone!

Peggy (*over this, begins to cry*) I knew nothing, I tell you! I promise to God! God help me, I swear!

> *The Soldier has gone to Hamilton to hold him back, shouting, 'Sir! Sir!' Hamilton stops shouting, steps back.*
> *Peggy collapses onto the ground and screams in pain. Hannah tries to comfort her. Between her screams, she whimpers, 'I'm innocent' over and over again.*

Hamilton (*to Soldier*) Double the guard for His Excellency. His life could be in danger.

> *Peggy suddenly lunges towards Hamilton, pulls his sword out of his belt and attempts to slit her own throat. Hannah screams, grabs the sword, cutting her hand. Hamilton pulls her away as the Soldier takes the sword. Peggy lies on the floor, trying to catch her breath, blood on her neck.*

Get her to bed.

Hannah She should see a doctor –

Hamilton Get her out of here!

> *Hannah helps Peggy up. They go out, though Peggy continues to wail and scream.*

(*to himself*) I hope to God she hangs.

Washington (*just off*) I thought we didn't believe in God.

> *Hamilton turns and Washington enters from the*

hallway. Pause.

She didn't know anything. Listen to her. That is the sound of a broken heart.

A scream off.

Such a man does not deserve a woman like that. And now she has to have his child. There is no justice.

Hamilton We should leave, sir.

Washington nods and sits.

Washington Why did he do it, Alexander? Why? (*Beat.*) His enemies are – nothing. Maggots. Compared to what he's fought. It is incomprehensible. (*He is lost in thought. Then*) They were arriving with our – spy. Have him brought in, Colonel.

Hamilton turns to leave.

(*stopping him*) I thought at least, I was a good judge of people.

Hamilton General –

Washington (*over him*) I shall never see him again. Shall I? Or even speak his name.

Washington, in the chair, closes his eyes. Hamilton hesitates, then hurries off.
Hannah enters, on her way through the room to the kitchen.
Washington opens his eyes.

(*to Hannah*) For the life of me, I can't recall a single prayer.

Hannah I'm getting her some water.

Washington You must know a prayer. Get me started.

Hannah hesitates, then nervously hurries out.
Washington sighs.
   Andre is brought in by a Soldier and Hamilton.
Andre's face is completely bloodied, and his clothes
torn.
   Washington does not look at him.

Andre Your Excellency. I wish to surrender to you.

   Beat.

Washington (*his mind elsewhere, not looking at Andre*)
To me?

Andre As an officer, sir.

Washington (*rubbing his eyes*) You're a spy. Look at you.

   Washington glances at Andre, but his mind for the rest
   of the scene is preoccupied.

Andre (*over this*) I'm a major in the British Army. Please.

Washington (*calmly*) Hang him.

Andre (*stunned*) I'm an officer in the British –!

Washington Hang him.

Andre I'm an officer, you can't –!

Hamilton Sir, there should be a hearing.

   Short pause. Washington remains completely
   distracted.

Washington First have the hearing, then hang him. Get
him out of here.

   Hamilton and the Soldier drag Andre out. He struggles
   and yells: 'You can't hang me! I'm a soldier, damn it!'
   etc.
   Alone Washington stands, and slowly follows them

*out, as Hannah enters with a pitcher of water and
hurries across the stage.*
   Upstairs, Peggy screams.

SCENE ELEVEN

New York City.
   *Sir Henry Clinton's office. Table and chairs. Mrs
Clinton, a woman in her fifties, sits to one side and sews.*
   *Arnold is shown in by Kemble, who then leaves. After a
moment, Sir Henry enters, all smiles.*

Sir Henry General Arnold, it is an honour. And a
pleasure.

   They shake hands.

Please, sit down. May I get you something to drink?

Arnold No, thank you.

   *Arnold sits. Pause. Sir Henry looks at Arnold and
smiles.*

Sir Henry (*finally*) Pity about what happened. It was such
an exciting prospect.

Arnold I did my best. If *The Vulture* had not anchored so
close to shore, then my men wouldn't have fired and –

Sir Henry I understand. Of course. (*Beat.*) Our mistake.
(*Beat.*) We dumb English.

Arnold I didn't say –

Sir Henry You Americans are so much more professional
at war than we are.

   *Short pause. He looks to his wife, who is impassive,
then back to Arnold.*

75

(*explaining*) My wife.

Arnold How do you do?

She says nothing, just nods and sews.

Sir Henry (*sighs, then*) I haven't slept since . . . (*He gestures to Arnold – 'Since your incident,' he means.*) They've put you up appropriately, I assume.

Arnold I'm comfortable.

Sir Henry You feel that a man of your stature is being treated fairly?

Arnold I'm comfortable.

Sir Henry I wouldn't want to hear you complain.

Arnold I'm not. I haven't.

Sir Henry (*suddenly changing the topic*) How well did you know Major Andre?

Arnold I only met –

Sir Henry (*over this*) I know you'd only met the once, but – how much did you know about him? About the sort of man he is? (*Beat.*) His profound sense of dignity. His manners. His grace. He's a poet, you know. Heroic, is how I've come to see him. When I close my eyes and see him.

Mrs Clinton turns for an instant to Sir Henry, then back to her sewing.

They've no right to murder such a man. He's a soldier for one. An officer. I'll fucking murder twenty rebels if they do.

Arnold Perhaps it's just a threat. They haven't killed him yet. (*Beat.*) I regret what happened. But again, had *The Vulture* anchored farther –

76

Sir Henry I'm pleased you agree with me – about John Andre. A fine . . . Look what a Mr Hamilton has sent. (*He holds up a letter.*) I gather he works for General Washington.

Arnold He does.

Sir Henry I gather he writes without the approval of – 'His Excellency'. He offers to release the Major.

Arnold Thank God.

Sir Henry In exchange for you.

Pause. Arnold just looks at Sir Henry.

I could never agree to such a trade, of course. How would it look – to return you . . . Who would ever defect again? That's true, isn't it?

There is no response.

And I cannot force you to do what is right.

Arnold Which is?

Sir Henry I can't say I've admired you, sir.

Arnold I don't understand.

Sir Henry To betray one's cause. Even a wrong and ghastly cause as the rebel's is. But you're a soldier, man! Where's your sense of honour, I ask myself. But then I'm not American, and I would be the first to say I don't begin to understand you Americans. (*Beat.*) What you value.

Arnold I've betrayed nothing – that has not already betrayed itself.

Sir Henry Is that right? Oh, I see. And so we do what we wish to do. Our consciences, is it? (*He smiles, then suddenly turns on him.*) And John Andre, a man I –

Mrs Clinton turns to hear this.

– admire, will be hanged because of you! Live with that!

Arnold (*incredulous*) Do you wish me to trade myself?

Short pause. No response.

You do, don't you? I do not believe this. I would think, in just pragmatic terms, my changing allegiances, would be of considerable –

Sir Henry I doubt it. I doubt if it matters. But if that is all which stands in your way of doing a very noble act –

Arnold They will kill me!

Sir Henry Yes. (*Beat.*) But you'd die comforted by the knowledge that you'd died nobly – having saved a good soul and a great man by your death. Think about it. It is worth thinking about.

Arnold I don't need to hear this –!

Sir Henry (*shouts*) Think about it, I said! And you'd better do just that, because I am the only hope you have now, you have no country, no home, no friends, no family, all you've got is me! (*Pause.*) Nobility, by the way, cannot be discussed in 'pragmatic terms'. At least I wouldn't know how. But perhaps you people have never understood that. You are so crude.

Arnold (*blurting out*) Major Andre promised me money –

Sir Henry Did he? Well go ask him about it! Sir, this may be America, but in this office at least it is still the King's country and here the world is not only about business and money. There is something greater. Something you in this Godforsaken piece of earth can't seem to understand! A decency! Virtue! And yes, honour! (*Beat.*) In my two years here, sir, I have searched with great interest to discover

78

what you Americans in fact believe in. Besides of course the freedom to cheat each other. I look in vain. Yours is a hollow race. Which, with each day – each new dawn, each new . . . (*He nods to Arnold.*) acquaintance, only disgusts me more. (*Short pause.*) He is a beautiful man. Andre.

Mrs Clinton puts down her sewing and listens to this.

Like a god.

Arnold He was drunk when we met –

Sir Henry I very much doubt that. A good *English* lad – worth, one would think, slightly more than a horde of your kind. That's my personal belief. My moral belief. (*Beat.*) For what it's worth. (*He smiles to Arnold.*) What do you have to live for, General Arnold? You've failed even us. You're despised – even by us. You think my soldiers will have anything but contempt for someone like you? (*He gestures to him.*) What is there to respect? So what is left? Sooner or later, you too will come to this conclusion. Why not sooner – and to save a life? (*Short pause.*) The Rebels have agreed to allow your wife, Peggy? – to join you here. (*Beat.*) She has refused. (*He hands Arnold Peggy's letter.*) She's chosen, she writes, to return to her family in Philadelphia, where she intends to seek an annulment of her marriage to the greatest scoundrel her young country has ever known. I don't think she's kidding.

Arnold looks at the letter.

She hates you . . . The list grows and grows. Trade yourself, damn it! Die with dignity not in some back room! Save a good man!

Major Kemble returns, his face now pale. He starts to speak, but can't.

(*impatient*) What? What?

Kemble (*holding in his hand a paper*) Major Andre – has been hanged (*He hands Sir Henry the paper. Pause*) I suggest we hang three prisoners this hour – our response. That we fucking cut off their heads and stick pikes through their skulls. (*Beat.*) Do I have your permission, sir?

Beat. Clinton, in a daze, nods.

It is said he died with honour. (*Beat.*) That rarely has a man faced death with such calm. Even Rebel officers – (*He nods towards the paper.*) – were seen to weep. His one regret, which he spoke just before his death, was that he was to be hanged, not shot, as is more appropriate for a gentleman. (*Beat.*) He died – like an Englishman.

Sir Henry holds his head in his hands. Kemble turns to Arnold.

Why don't you go?

Arnold hesitates, then:

Arnold Sir Henry, I wish to know if you intend to honour the financial arrangement agreed to by Major Andre. (*Beat.*) I have nothing. I was promised ten thousand pounds.

Sir Henry looks up at Arnold.

Sir Henry Get this scum out of my office! Get him out!

Sir Henry goes to draw his sword. Kemble holds him back. Sir Henry suddenly begins to moan and howl in great pain.
Mrs Clinton stands, sets down her sewing. Kemble tries to comfort Sir Henry.

Mrs Clinton (*to Kemble*) Take him to his bedroom. He should lie down.

Kemble helps Sir Henry off. He continues to moan.

(*to Arnold*) My husband – liked Major Andre very much.
That must be clear. (*Beat.*) He spent so much time with
him. He is – was – a charming man. A pleasure to be with.
So I'm told. My husband seemed always to be thinking
about him. He would say things – and I would know this.
That he was thinking of John. (*Beat.*) I was even a little
jealous.

Sir Henry moans, off.

I'll go and comfort him now. (*She nods to Arnold and
leaves.*)

*Arnold hesitates. Sir Henry howls 'John!', off, then
Arnold leaves the office.*

SCENE TWELVE

*New York City. Sitting room of Arnold's temporary
residence. Table, chairs. Hannah sits with a Mr Robinson,
a 20-year-old American Loyalist; they are just finishing
tea.*

Hannah (*in the middle of a story*) I hadn't known this, but
my brother had already told this man, two or three times,
that he'd best stay away from me.

Robinson (*very interested*) This was the Frenchman.

Hannah Yes. Now I knew that General Arnold hated
French people.

Robinson Who doesn't. The other day I heard a joke
about the French, it was very funny. Very true. I wish I
could remember it.

Hannah (*as an afterthought*) And he loved the English.

Robinson (*as if the most obvious thing in the world*) Of course!

Hannah But my Frenchman was so handsome!

She and Robinson laugh at this.

And I was – I wasn't always old.

Robinson starts to say a compliment.

Don't say a word. I'm not asking for lies.

Robinson It was not a lie I was about to speak.

She looks at him, smiles.

Hannah But – it was our money the Frenchman was after. My brother told me this later. We had a lot of property. We were society – in New Haven.

Robinson nods.

Robinson That means something, I know.

Hannah So on one of my Frenchman's visits to me, Benedict arrives with a friend at the front door, asks his friend to knock and he, my brother, goes out back and hides in the bushes –

Arnold enters. Robinson immediately stands and smiles.

Robinson Sir, it is an honour.

He holds out his hand to shake, Arnold takes it. He turns to Hannah.

Hannah Mr Robinson. He has an uncle with a house – where is it in London?

Robinson The Brompton Road.

Hannah That's supposed to be a very nice area. Lots of Americans live there. There's still a little tea –

Arnold shakes his head. Then sits. Robinson sits back down, not knowing what to say.

Let me just finish my story. So the General is out back in the bushes. My suitor – (*to Arnold*) the French boy – hearing someone coming in the front door, suddenly throws open a window and jumps out – into the arms of – him. And then you whipped him, right? (*Beat.*) He's always protected me. (*She takes Arnold's hand. Short awkward pause.*)

Robinson (*finally, to Arnold*) We admired very much what you attempted to achieve, General. It's a pleasure to have a man like yourself on our side.

Arnold looks at Robinson, who sips his tea.

Hannah Mr Robinson comes from – how far north of Albany is that?

Robinson (*to Arnold*) You probably know the estate. It's quite a sizeable tract –

Arnold (*over this*) *That* Robinson, yes. And there was a beautiful manse –

Robinson (*over this*) I was born in that house!

Arnold Were you? It's gone now –

Robinson I've been told that –

Arnold I burned it down. (*Beat.*) Not me, personally. On my orders. While retreating from Quebec. Quite the manse. It was in the way. But now, as you say, we're on the same side. (*Arnold stands and holds out his hand.*) Perhaps we'll meet some day on the Brompton Road, Mr Robinson.

Robinson hesitates, then realizes he is being told the tea is over. He stands and shakes hands.

Hannah Mr Robinson, it was a pleasure. At last – some intelligent conversation! (*She smiles.*)

Robinson Thank you – for the tea. I should go. I'm expected . . . General – God save the King. I'll show myself out. (*He goes.*)

Hannah I am trying to make friends.

Arnold has looked at his pocket watch.

She's late. Does that surprise you?

There is no response.

There's another account in this morning's paper from Philadelphia.

Arnold I've read enough accounts –

Hannah It appears not only did she denounce you publicly, she walked in the procession –

Arnold (*yells over this*) I don't want to know!

Hannah (*newspaper in hand*) This isn't love!

Arnold She's a child.

Hannah No she isn't.

Arnold She did what she had to – to survive. They made her. She made a mistake.

Hannah Is that why she's coming here – to survive? Is that enough for you?

She has hurt him. Short pause.

I just don't want you hurt, that is all. You make your bed, you lie in it, you don't keep trying to wiggle out. That's what I can't abide.

Arnold I know what you can't abide, Hannah! Now be quiet!

The doorbell rings, off.
  Beat.
  It rings again.

Hannah I'll go. (*She starts, then turns back.*) I have stood with you, brother. I never – questioned. (*Beat.*) That is what love is. I'll get the door. (*She goes.*)

  Off, the sound of a baby crying. Arnold sits and waits.
  After a moment, Peggy, no longer pregnant, enters, taking off her hat. They look at each other. The baby cries, off.

Arnold Hannah doesn't know babies. Maybe you should . . .

Peggy She'll do fine.

  Beat.

Arnold (*referring to the baby*) Is that – ours?

  She nods.

How was the journey? Would you like to sit down?

  She shakes her head.

(*He gestures to the room.*) I tried to make it as comfortable as possible. I hope you approve, Peggy. (*Pause.*) I am very sorry you were not allowed to remain in Philadelphia.

  She shrugs.

Peggy (*as if explaining*) The wife of Benedict Arnold . . . Even the innocent wife. Or so most believed –

  He reaches for her hand.

Arnold Sit down, sit down.

  The baby stops crying.

85

I want to see him.

Peggy Yes. (*She sits.*)

Arnold I can try to find you a different house to stay in, should you not wish – should you wish to be alone.

Peggy (*not answering*) It's comfortable. Your sister's done an admirable job.

   Short pause.

Arnold You look splendid.

Peggy (*laughs*) No, I don't. (*She looks into his face.*) You are the most hated man – ever. I don't understand. (*She looks away.*) I was forced to watch them drag a likeness –

Arnold (*trying to stop her*) I read about –

Peggy (*over this*) A likeness of you, through the streets, dragged by a rope around its neck. The screams of people. What they said. (*She shakes her head.*) I attacked you. Someone put a club in my hand, so I hit. I marched with them. Someone called out, spit on him! (*Beat.*) So I spat – on you. (*Beat.*) I thought then they'd let me stay. (*Beat.*) I'm very sorry.

   He looks at her.

Arnold I make no judgement. How can I?

Peggy They burned you – a face on each side of a head. Two faces?

   He nods, he understands.

With horns. My family's all denounced you. And when we were told I'd have to leave, what could they do? They begged. (*She shrugs.*)

Arnold And why do they think I did it?

86

Peggy Who?

Arnold (*shrugs*) Your family –

Peggy (*quickly*) For money.

He closes his eyes.

That's the reason everybody gives. You were paid ten
thousand pounds by –

Arnold I haven't gotten it, I've asked –

Peggy Then you did want money?

Arnold For a reimbursement – my pay – what I'd – I was
owed – (*He looks at her.*) Forget it. I made a deal with
Andre. Nothing's in writing.

Peggy For some reason, he's become a hero, Andre. They
say he died so – well. I've tried to explain to my sisters that
he's an actor –

Arnold (*realizing*) Of course! That's why –

Peggy But, now he's a hero. It makes no sense. Nothing
does. I hate this country. May it rot in hell. May it sink to
the bottom of the ocean. I felt so used! Who the hell do
they think they are? I don't know what they see that's so
good! (*She almost cries, but stops herself.*) The things
people are made to do. I love my father. He is my father.
That's his crime. Now they must humiliate him. (*Beat.*) I'd
like to stay here with my husband.

He looks at her.

Until we sail together. London will be so grand, Benedict! I
see it already. The theatres, the shops. I've seen etchings –
you've already been –

Arnold I was a boy!

Peggy (*continuing*) And I think there can't be any place

87

better. I think we're lucky. That's what I told my sister. You'll be respected. After what you've done. Like you must be respected here by the British. Giving you this house. And ten thousand pounds!

He watches her.

And then we'll win the war and come back, and then we'll see who has a carriage. We'll see who's made to spit on whose husband! (*She starts to weep.*) Oh Benedict.

He goes and hugs her.

I'm so frightened. I want to go home.

Pause as they hug.

Arnold Peggy? One of the charges against me? (*He tries to get her attention.*) That the Committee made against me? They said I profited by letting a ship – giving it a pass. (*Beat.*) I did . . . profit. I did own a share.

She looks at him.

I did that.

Short pause.

Peggy (*incredulous*) So what? (*then on to a new subject*) God knows what I'll miss. What do you think you'll miss?

He shrugs.

Arnold There's probably – some smell? That a country has, that you don't even notice while you're there but you notice it when it's gone. (*Beat.*) Probably some – fertile smell. I don't know. (*He takes deep breaths, trying to calm himself.*) We've been offered passage – next week.

Suddenly, off, the baby begins to cry again. They listen.

I don't even know his name. It is a –?

She nods. Beat.

Peggy (*then*) George.

He looks at her.

After the King.

*This makes him suddenly laugh, and the laugh is
enough to break him and he begins to sob.*
The baby cries, off.
*Peggy watches her husband. Then she stands and
helps him up.*

Peggy Come on. He needs you to hold him. And comfort
him.

They go off.
The baby continues to cry.

SCENE THIRTEEN

*Twenty-one years later; June, 1801. Churchyard of St
Mary's, Battersea, London.*
*Four men carry on a coffin. One of them is 20, and
wears a British Army uniform. He is George. Behind him
come Hannah, Peggy, a Minister, and a woman hired from
the church choir.*
*The coffin is set down, and the Minister begins. The
sound of wind mixes with his prayer.*

Minister O God, whose mercies cannot be numbered:
Accept our prayers on behalf of your servant, Benedict,
and grant him an entrance into the land of light and joy, in
the fellowship of your saints; through Jesus Christ our
Lord, who lives and reigns with you and the Holy Spirit,
one God, now and for ever. Amen.

All Amen.

George steps forward to say a few words over the grave.

George Marooned is how Father sometimes put it, marooned upon a distant shore, so far from home . . .

Suddenly the shouts and noise of a full session of Congress are heard.
   A lone Representative takes the floor and begins to cry out.

Man Mr Speaker! Mr Speaker!

The funeral service continues and George's words continue, though unheard; so the stage now represents two places: the graveyard, and the floor of the House of Representatives, Washington, DC.

Mr Speaker!

A gavel is heard pounding, and the noise from the house dips.

May I have the floor, please!

More gavel pounding, then:

Thank you. Gentlemen, I have an announcement. (*He holds up a letter.*) It is my pleasure to report to this body – the death of Benedict Arnold in London.

A stirring is heard.

The most heinous man America has known – is dead at last!

Cheers.

It is reported that our embassy received a request from the family to bring the body back here. (*Shouts of* 'No', *etc.*). That request was quickly denied! (*Cheers.*) And relish the news that he died in penury and squalor, hated and shunned by all decent men of all nations. A just reward, is it not? (*Beat.*) May his be a lesson for all traitors. That God watches over America. He watches over us. With this just death, we all may breathe easier and with the knowledge that America is safer, one enemy is no more. (*Beat.*) How comforting it is too, in times like our own when daily the world looms diffuse and vague, to be reminded of a simple unassailable truth: there is justice. There is right and wrong. There is good – and there is evil. (*Beat.*) God bless America!

> *The entire chamber of the House of Representatives shouts out: 'God bless America.'*
> *Suddenly the noise of the house, and the Man who was speaking, are gone. All that remains is the graveyard, and George finishing his words . . .*

George . . . without regret, without complaint, is how Father lived these twenty years. A proud soldier. A general – from America. (*Beat.*) Battersea, we know, is not where he wished to lie. But here we are. So far away. (*He goes and touches the coffin.*) Now it's time to sleep.

> *Peggy hands George a wrapped package.*

Peggy George . . .

> *He takes it, unwraps the brown paper, and takes out an American flag. He goes and silently wraps it over the coffin, and then stands back.*
> *The Woman from the church choir steps forward and begins to sing Psalm 13 (in a version from the American Ainsworth Psalter).*

Woman (*sings*)
How long, Jehovah,
wilt Thou me forget
fore 'er?
How long will Thou hide
Thy face from me away?

How long shall in my soul,
I consult daily
sad sorrow in my heart?
How long shall my foe be
exalted over me?

Curtain.